PENGUIN BOOKS

HOW YOU CAN LEARN TO LIVE WITH COMPUTERS

Harry Kleinberg, a computer engineer, works for the RCA Corporation and lives in Cherry Hill, New Jersey, with his wife and three children.

How You Can Learn to Live with COMPUTERS

Harry Kleinberg

PENGUIN BOOKS

Penguin Books Ltd, Harmondsworth,
Middlesex, England
Penguin Books, 625 Madison Avenue,
New York, New York 10022, U.S.A.
Penguin Books Australia Ltd, Ringwood,
Victoria, Australia
Penguin Books Canada Limited, 2801 John Street,
Markham, Ontario, Canada L3R 1B4
Penguin Books (N.Z.) Ltd, 182–190 Wairau Road,
Auckland 10, New Zealand

First published in the United States of America by
J. B. Lippincott Company 1977
Published in Penguin Books 1978

LIBRARY OF CONGRESS CATALOGING IN PUBLICATION DATA
Kleinberg, Harry.
How you can learn to live with computers.
Includes index.
1. Computers. 2. Computer engineering. I. Title.
QA76.K527 1978 001.6'4 78-17449
ISBN 0 14 00.4970 3

Printed in the United States of America by
Offset Paperback Mfrs., Inc., Dallas, Pennsylvania
Set in Electra

To NELL, ALLAN, DEBRA, and SARAH,
and to all the computer engineers I've known—
I learned something from every one of them

Contents

How You Can Learn to Live with
COMPUTERS

Prologue: A Personal Perspective

BEING a computer engineer is neither illegal nor immoral. It isn't even something to be ashamed of, I guess, but there was a time in my life when I was reluctant to admit that I was one. The confession created all sorts of problems. Consider, for example, the simple, friendly ritual of meeting people at a cocktail party. A standard part of the ceremonial is to be asked, "And what do you do?" The simple response, "I design digital computers," usually turned out to have a dramatically chilling effect. When computers were still very new, people reacted as though they had just been introduced to a specimen from another world and seemed unable to find an appropriate response.

As computers became more common, attitudes changed but, sadly, not for the better. "Yeah? Well, there's some functions girls perform around the office that no machine will ever do, haw, haw, haw." "My sister-in-law was laid off when her company put in one of those machines." "Why can't you technicians leave well enough alone and stop puttering with those dangerous gadgets?"

All in all, the social price for doing that kind of work was higher than it deserved to be. Computer designers are people, after all. In fact, some of my best friends are computer engineers, and I wouldn't really mind if my daughter married one. They are even a fairly normal bunch, although their normality does differ a bit from other people's. They come in a variety of shapes, several colors, and a wide range of temperaments. Their backgrounds are diverse, their political views and life styles are varied, but not a single one of them has supernatural powers.

This runs counter to the general impression that computers were born in a dark, cluttered laboratory, fathered by impassive wizards puttering around a boiling cauldron. From their labors a sinister entity, half electronic and half human, sprang into being. Surely those who are privileged to know these mysterious creations must be initiated into some secret cult and possess powers beyond those of a mere mortal.

Not so. The designers are people with ordinary powers and ordinary limitations. Although most of them are bright, genius is as rare among them as among any other group of talented people. Back in the early and middle 1950s, when the machines were young and of unproven practicality, the people trying to make them into producible devices did include a higher than usual percentage of oddballs. The novelty of the work seemed to attract a zany, highly individual kind of guy who followed whatever impulses possessed him at the moment, without any interest in how his actions might look to others. Their eccentricities showed in little things, like wearing half-unfastened fleece-lined flying boots all the time, no matter what the season of the year or how formal the occasion, or jumping on top of a desk and thumping the chest like Tarzan when a tough problem was solved.

While they all qualified as normal, at least by their own definition of the term, by no means were they all made to the same pattern. They came from all over the world, their educational backgrounds ranged from anthropology to nuclear physics, and a substantial number had either dropped out of, or never attended, a university. So varied were they that during all that early period I could find only two characteristics that could be called common.

One was that they all liked puzzles and were very good at solving them. (I include as puzzles such games as chess and bridge.) Any kind of puzzle would satisfy the lust, as long as it was intellectually challenging and had absolutely no practical value. Solutions had to be worked out only for the sake of showing that they could be found.

The other common factor was that they were universally bad at arithmetic. They could never be trusted to add up a column of numbers or to multiply anything by anything and have more than a random chance of getting the right answer. (I refuse to editorialize on what this might signify.)

By now, though, the situation has calmed down. Computer Science has been taught in universities for many years, but only after having been made almost impossible to understand and completely unexciting, as befits the subject of a college course. The design of the machines, while it can still be done either creatively or unimaginatively, has become a fairly straightforward problem, with a lot of precedent to fall back on. The engineers who are now in the business are completely typical engineers, and I doubt that a college dropout could get a job in the field today.

Just as computer experts come from the same genetic sources as the rest of us, so do the machines have a common heritage with all our other machines. The computer's ancestors are to be found in the same long line of discovery and invention that spawned washing machines and radios and any number of other familiar machines and gadgets.

Neither are the more immediate technological forebears of computers a very exotic group. From the development of radar in the 1930s and 1940s came a deeper understanding of how to work with short pulses of electrical energy. From the nuclear research of the same period came electronic circuits to keep track of what was going on inside the atom, circuits that were direct forerunners of many of those used in computers. And from the rapidly developing telephone systems of the 1930s came the knowledge of how to organize large numbers of switching elements into massive, complex systems. So computers are not a departure from past technology, but a consequence of it. No new laws of physics were discovered, nor were any old ones repealed, to make them practical.

But technology was not the only thing needed before computers could be developed; there also had to be the desire to make them. Here, too, there is no lack of background, because the human race has always behaved as though it has an instinctive and hereditary dislike for arithmetic. It's as if we figured out one morning how to add and subtract and on the afternoon of the same day started looking for some contraption to relieve us of the drudgery this new skill turned out to be. From the earliest days of mathematics, clever people who hated to add or multiply racked their brains to figure out how to use the technology of their day to perform the loathsome task. In fact, if you classify piling up stones as a mechanical aid, there is a strong possibility that gadgetry preceded the theoretical knowledge of arithmetic.

But despite the computer's long and respectable background, its appearance on the scene evoked a startled reaction from most people, as though a menacing figure had crept up behind them in the darkness and suddenly yelled, "Boo!" This was probably the result of bad timing. The period around World War II, during which the computer was born, was a difficult time for so specialized a machine to get much attention. It was totally overshadowed by two other technologies that burst into sight at the same time: atomic energy and space exploration. These were highly visible developments whose implications could be grasped and debated, and upon which positions could be taken by most people. There is nothing very subtle about the purpose of a megaton bomb. There is nothing hard to explain about the courage needed to sit on top of a blazing rocket.

The computer, however, was much less conspicuous. It was accompanied by no mushroom clouds or vaporized islands. It did not have a Cape Canaveral with a succession of dramatic countdowns. Instead, the early computers were tools for scientists and mathematicians to use in back rooms for specialized work which nobody else understood. So only a small percentage of the population even heard of the computer during the first dozen years of its existence. The first one that I ever saw was one I helped to build.

Unfortunately, when public awareness of the computer did come, it was to the accompaniment of a great deal of hoopla. Electronic Brains had finally arrived! The Thinking Machine was here! And that kind of talk was hard to disbelieve. After all, the atomic bomb and the rocket ship had just turned Buck Rogers from fantasy to reality overnight; why shouldn't the same thing happen with this other old science-fiction theme?

Very little has happened to dispel this early excitement and overenthusiasm. As the public's contact with computers began to grow, through utility bills, magazine subscriptions, classroom scheduling, and so on, the blunders that periodically came to light smudged the image of the machine's infallibility but did little to remove its mystery. People generally still don't know how computers work or what their limitations are.

Nor did it help that, from the very beginning, the experts have written about what the computer might some day become, without ever making clear exactly what it is now. The result has been a general confusion between actuality and potential, between the realities of today and the maybes of tomorrow.

All these factors led to the creation of many myths about the computer, which is unfortunate because myths can lead you astray when you have no way of comparing them with reality. And many of the most common ideas about computers fall into the category of things that are simply not true. In some cases fact and fancy are separated merely by the use of an old word in a new and unexplained context, but whatever the cause may be, the situation is one that should be remedied.

Adding still further to the confusion has been the orchestration of public statements by the technical prophets. On one side of the platform the trumpets of artificial intelligence blare out the imminent arrival of the new age of liberation: mental drudgery will be as outmoded as physical labor; social decisions will be made with speed and correctness. But the sad cellos on the other side of the stage predict the darkening shadow of human subjugation: mankind is doomed to become a digitized, nameless mass whose every action and thought are known to the Machine, and those who control the Machine will control us all.

The only way to sort out the conflicting prophecies and to separate myth from fact is to learn something about how computers work. That isn't as difficult as it is sometimes made out to be. You don't have to study binary numbers or Boolean algebra or learn how to design a shift register, because the function of a machine can be understood and evaluated without that kind of specialized knowledge. For example, suppose you drive a car across a bridge and get caught by a police radar unit for speeding. You can fully comprehend the situation without knowing anything about the Carnot cycle, Young's modulus, or the Doppler effect, because you understand what the car, the bridge, and the radar set can and can't do.

You can learn that much about computers too. You can, in fact, even qualify to enter the debate as to whether or not they are machines that think. You don't have to have a doctorate in psychology or a private lab at MIT to be able to make judgments of your own on a subject that has had more mystique built up around it than it deserves.

The formula for reaching that level of knowledge is basically simple: you just learn how the elementary parts of the machine work. There is no need to tangle with the highly complex structure of the finished computer, which takes a lot of time and concentration. All the important characteristics of the computer flow from the nature of its components.

The reluctance to get down into the guts of the computer may partly reflect the modern style of tackling problems. It has become most chic to claim that you are concerned with the overall view, looking at the big picture, seeing the forest instead of the trees. And while that is exactly the kind of view you want to end with, you must master a certain amount of detail before you can understand the whole. After all, how well can one really judge a forest without knowing the difference between a spruce and a maple? Do overall views make any sense unless you can tell land from water, meadow from marsh?

The detail needed to understand the computer is not beyond the grasp of the nonexpert, because the chief clue is not an engineering subject. The significance of the computer is not based on the esoterica of circuit design or information theory, but rather on the nature of logic. In fact, the first step into the bowels of the computer is to recognize one simple fact: it has been given the wrong name. It should have been called "the logic machine."

The differentiation is important because logic is the source both of the machine's capabilities and of its limitations. The ability to perform logically is the area in which the machine and the human mind overlap and is thus the basis of the arguments about whether the computer thinks. To understand the uses and misuses of logic is to understand the computer.

The best road to that understanding starts with a quick look at the "big picture," in order to assess the subject in broad terms. But this should be followed at once by a descent into the working depths of the machine where the logical elements are. Having mastered those fundamentals, you can then reascend to look at the grand view with a better understanding of what you are seeing and a better ability to place in perspective anything you might hear about the computer in the future. If along the way we can stake out the limits of the machine as an artificial intelligence, so much the better.

There is also a bonus as part of the package. Having come to see the computer in its real role as a logic machine, you will be able to see how much of your own job the computer will ever be able to do. If you've always wanted to know how you personally stack up against the computer, here's your chance to find out. If you like the result, you'll be happy to find that there is someone who understands you. If you don't like it, you can simply shrug off the theory as the mindless rambling of one who knows not whereof he speaks.

1

The Three Faces

WHEN I saw my first Cubist painting I had no idea that it was a picture of a woman holding a guitar. If my friend the expert had not taken pity on my ignorance, I still wouldn't know.

"Look, stupid," he said, in effect, "can't you see what the artist is doing? These shapes are from the guitar, and these are from the woman, and these are from the table. He reduced all the complicated forms to the simplest squares and circles and rearranged them."

"But what about all those shapes that are left over?"

"They show how the subject would look if you could see it from different angles at the same time. He's presenting several views on the same canvas."

As I followed him meekly to the next picture, discretion kept me from pointing out that architects and engineers also show several views, but much more neatly and clearly.

I have never felt that the Cubists' technique is a good one, but, oddly, their way of looking at the world is probably the best route to an understanding of the computer. It certainly should be reduced to its most basic elements, and it certainly should be seen from several sides at the same time.

Like many other machines, the computer has more than

one face. All the faces are real, and it is important not to lose sight of any of them. It is tempting and easy to approach any modern technology from one side only and to decide that it is evil or benevolent, oppressive or uplifting. It is also misleading and unrealistic to do so. The computer, for example, presents to the world at least three faces; you could point to any one of them and say, "That's what a computer looks like," and be telling part of the truth. However, if you want an accurate perspective of the machine, you must recognize all of them, but clearly and neatly, as an architect or engineer would show them.

The first face of the computer is the impressive one, the subject of the ooh-ing and ah-ing in the Sunday supplements and the television documentaries. Most of the awe and wonder is well deserved. Computers are remarkable and very important fruits of technology, surely among the most significant of them all. They are made up of ridiculously simple elements, but they contain so many of them, so intricately interconnected, that the finished machines are exceedingly complex. As a result, they are difficult to explain in a simple and organized fashion, which is one reason they have remained objects of mystery.

In addition, they operate in an area that had been for centuries the sole preserve of relatively educated specialists. After all, the ability to work with complex mathematics is not very widely distributed among the world's population. That makes it hard to explain exactly why the machines have been so useful to scientists.

To compound the wonder, the versatility of computers is unprecedented. The same machine can be used to guide travel in space, to sniff out errors in tax returns, to control city traffic, to design camera lenses, to keep track of telephone bills, and on and on.

But, above all, computers are unbelievably fast Their

most impressive and most important characteristic is their speed, so great that it is difficult to measure in terms you can relate to your own experience. It doesn't help to quote figures about microseconds or thousands of operations per second; these are just abstract numbers with no real meaning. So are the standard comparisons between yourself and the computer; even a small computer can polish off in a few seconds all the arithmetic you will ever do, from the day you learn to count until the moment you deposit your last pension check. Your whole lifetime of calculation is reduced to a few ticks of the clock, but even that doesn't fully convey the message. The point is important because the speed at which the computer works is not just a gimmick, nor is it the blind pursuit of "more, bigger, faster"; it is the key to the significance of the machine. Its speed becomes the crowbar for prying open problems that can be tackled in no other way.

Unfortunately it is also the source of one of the most prevalent misstatements about computers—namely, that they do things which it is impossible for people to do by themselves. Be careful with those words. Computers don't do anything people couldn't do if the speed element were removed. They do things which are impossible for people to do in a given time. They don't actually deal with the impossible at all; what they do is make impractical tasks practical.

I recognize that the difference between impossible and impractical is elusive, especially in talking about something as poorly understood as the computer. But you can make a valid analogy with another kind of impressive machinery—earth-moving equipment. I never miss a chance to watch those huge machines that enable one man to lift, move, tamp, and push unbelievably large quantities of earth. They amplify human strength to an unprecedented degree, literally making it possible for a man to move mountains. They do impossible jobs in exactly the same sense as the computer does.

For example, consider the Great Wall of China, reaching for thousands of miles over prairie, mountains, forest, desert; as high as a three-story building, as wide as a two-lane highway. Imagine undertaking a project on that scale without trucks, bulldozers, or electrical equipment of any kind, using only the most basic and primitive hand tools. We know it is impossible. Yet we also know that it has been done.

Power equipment, like the computer, turns the impractical into the practical. We could build our entire national highway system without using any modern machinery. The only difference would be that 90 percent of the time required would be taken up by physical labor, and 10 percent by the bureaucratic preparation. Machinery makes it possible to reverse these figures.

A similar situation exists in the mathematical world, where a great many complex problems in science and engineering have theoretical solutions that have been known for a long time. But these solutions are usually in the form of differential equations, about which it need only be said that they are a subdivision of the general subject of calculus, and that they consist of a lot of *x*'s and *y*'s connected by some very exotic symbols. While mathematicians are satisfied that they have solved a problem when they write down a set of complicated equations, the engineer feels differently. When he or she tries to turn those equations into numerical answers for a specific, practical case, they lead to an incredible tangle of arithmetic. The number of adds, subtracts, multiplies, and divides runs quickly into the tens and hundreds of thousands, sometimes into the millions. Doing them by hand, or even with desk calculators, would take time measured in days, months, or even years. It was always possible to do the work, in the sense that people knew exactly what had to be done, but until the computer became available, it was totally impractical.

In certain cases, however, "doing the impossible" is a

much more justified phrase. These are cases in which the speed of the computer is absolutely critical. For example, the equations which describe the movement of bodies in outer space go back about three hundred years to Sir Isaac Newton. If you were navigating a space ship to the moon, it would be possible for you to solve those equations to find out where you were going to land; the only trouble is that it would take you hours or days to work out the answers. In a moon landing, you can't wait hours or days, you need the answers right now, and only a computer can do the job in the time available.

Even when an immediate solution is not the major consideration, don't underestimate the importance of making this kind of mathematical work practical. The computer's availability as a tool to cope with staggeringly complex calculations has had a tremendous impact on every aspect of science and engineering. Its utility in organizing vast amounts of data has opened up entire new areas of use by business and by government. It has become an indispensable tool in any kind of work involving large quantities of information, and that means almost every field of human interest. We may have mixed feelings about the eventual value of these uses, but we cannot question their significance.

The second face is a comic one that has been seen by relatively few who are not directly involved with computers. I have a very high regard for those nontechnical people who have been able to see inside the infallible robot to find the buffoonery underneath. It takes a very sharp insight to recognize, without an intimate knowledge of the anatomy of the machine, that behind its façade of flawless functioning is a rich lode of comedy waiting to be explored: computers, and the way they are used, contain a very large element of the absurd.

There is, for instance, an uncanny resemblance between

computers and bureaucrats. Anyone who has dealt with a minor official who uses a book of rules as a substitute for a brain will have no trouble seeing the similarity. The official and the computer share the same exasperating trait of following instructions to the letter in a completely automatic way: an instruction exists to be followed, no matter how grotesque the result may be. A computer sends out a bill for $0.00 and, when there is no response, prints out increasingly nasty reminders. It is pacified only when a payment of $0.00 has been recorded. A government clerk requires that a one-year-old child sign a loyalty oath on an immigration visa and is pacified only when the space on the form contains a signature, any signature. The computer sends the bill because the programmer didn't properly "instruct" it for the case of a zero balance. The clerk requires the signature because his book of procedures didn't properly "instruct" him for the case of the child. They are brothers under the skin. But there is an even stronger bond between them—a bond of paper.

I've heard the times we live in referred to as the atomic age, the age of dissent, or the communications age. Nonsense, this is the age of paper. Our most important national resource is not electricity or petroleum or minerals, but typewriter ribbons. If anyone in government is concerned about the possible subversion of our system, he shouldn't worry about the security of power plants or water supplies—that's old-fashioned. But the stationery stores across the country should be guarded day and night, because not a single segment of our society could operate without putting little marks on pieces of paper. Even those who claim they want to destroy the system arm themselves early with paper, typewriters, and copying machines.

The heroic figure of our time is the scribe, and the computer is his ultimate weapon. It is to him what Excalibur was to King Arthur, the mirrored shield to Perseus. Just as those weapons gave their owners strength and power far beyond the limits of ordinary men, so does the computer magnify the capabilities of the scribe. In his chosen task of putting words to paper, it lifts him to a level of potency that his predecessors could not have imagined in their wildest dreams, since attached to almost every computer is something called a high-speed printer, a name that is well deserved. These monstrous typewriters can routinely grind out 1,200 lines of print in a minute. Every line can contain about 120 characters. That comes to a printing capability of 144,000 characters per minute per printer. In the United States alone, the number of such printers is in the tens of thousands. So when you multiply, you find that in an eight-hour day . . . Do the rest of the arithmetic yourself; my mind has already boggled. In case you want bigger numbers, the paper forms used in these printers have built-in carbon paper, so that five or six copies of everything they print can be made at one time.

What happens to all this paper? It gets distributed to people. There are, in most organizations that use computers, messengers whose job it is to haul these stacks of paper out to the proper offices. They roam the corridors with carts overflowing with the massive output of the machine, delivering it in strict accordance with carefully regulated distribution lists: this two-foot stack to the accounting section, that one to production control, the next to purchasing. What these people do with the print-outs I haven't the foggiest idea, but they certainly aren't able to read them. They hardly have time to turn all the pages before the next stack is delivered.

I remember one manager shaking his head in dismay at a freshly printed pile that must have numbered over a thousand pages. "All I wanted," he said sadly, "was a little bit of information. You ask that damned machine for a drink of water and it hits you in the face with a five-inch hose."

Every time I meet my old colleague Eddie, he reminds

me how prophetic he was in the 1950s. "One day," he used to predict, "the United States will have to make friends with China. That's the only way we'll ever get enough people to read all the stuff these machines can print."

In general, you can define computer output as a very large mass of paper that passes through a high-speed printer on its way from the factory to the incinerator. The problem has been recognized by most people who deal with the machines, but no one has yet come up with an adequate answer. The most likely solution appears to lie in small television-like units which make it possible for you to see the information you wanted from the computer, read it, and erase the screen. Such devices have been available for several years, but their cost is only now coming down to the point of economic practicality. In the meantime, the people who operate the computers shrug their shoulders, feed the paper into the printers, and try to get the best price they can from the paper-recycling companies.

While the impressive and the comic aspects of the computer are very real, so is its third face—the sinister one. Concern about this aspect has many facets, ranging from such abstractions as the relationship of man and machine to the practical economic problems of automation and unemployment. But focus for the moment on the possible threat at the personal level.

It has to be recognized that computers have very dangerous potential. Their impressive power is not restricted to making up a payroll or designing better brakes for cars. There are ways they can be used that could lead to extremely unhappy consequences for all of us. Of these, the most significant is the well-publicized data bank, about which most of the fuss is currently being made. While this is a complex subject, the basics are not difficult to state.

An important feature of the computer is the provision for storing data for future use. One of the ways this is done is by magnetic recording on various forms of tape or disks. With these devices a great deal of information can be stored compactly and relatively cheaply and, most important, is easily and quickly accessible through the computer. Many systems in use today can store the equivalent of about one hundred million words, with access to any of them in about one twentieth of a second. There is absolutely no doubt that these figures will be greatly improved in the near future.

The collection of data stored in this form is called the data base or data bank of the system. Almost every application of a computer requires one of these, although most of them are neither so large nor so fast as those figures might indicate. Much of the time they hold such routine business records as warehouse inventories, engineering documents, airline reservations, and so on, none of which presents any problem to most of us. But we do have a major concern with the use of data banks, especially by governments, to store information about ourselves.

Here again, the computer does nothing that hasn't been done before, and you can make a superficial case for the "no need to worry about it" school of thought. After all, governments have kept records about their citizens for centuries. The census has been with us forever, and tax rolls go as far back into history as any form of writing lets us see. Records are not something that suddenly happened when the computer was invented. Indeed, some records, such as Social Security, are kept at our own insistence. Besides, the mere fact that a government keeps track of its citizens has not automatically meant oppression.

But the point is that, if a government should be inclined toward oppression, information about people becomes a very important tool. Until now, such files and dossiers have always been segmented, hard to coordinate, difficult of access, and subject to all the errors and confusion of any big clerical job. Inefficiency, which has dangers of its own, has helped save us from too much control.

The computer data bank is still only a filing system, but a superbly fast and efficient one. It is an excellent example of the way the speed of the computer, applied to an old practice, can introduce problems of an entirely new kind. Once information is entered into this system, it is there, consistently accessible at the touch of the proper buttons, retrievable at any hour, never misfiled, never lost. No more foul-ups, no more delays, no more confusion.

In addition, the information is stored in what is basically an electrical form, which means that it can easily be linked up with any of the "electric media," as Marshall McLuhan would call them. The data bank can be connected to telephone, telegraph, or radio systems, making the data in the file available anywhere those links exist, which is practically everywhere. Add the fact that orbiting communication satellites are now a reality, and you can see how the data bank can easily become part of a global network. It is completely practical to have a file containing information about as many people as you care to keep track of. The file could be queried from any place in the world and a dossier on anybody obtained in a matter of seconds.

Information about people has never before been so quickly available to government, or to anybody else who is given access to the file. The consequences, if such a system were built, are hard to predict. But remember that George Orwell wrote *1984* before the day of the computer. Imagine the kind of book it would have been had he known about global data banks. The Gestapo operated very efficiently without this kind of system. What could they have done had they had one?

It is important not to become frozen with fear by this potentially ominous face of the computer, any more than you should be struck blind with awe at its wizardry, or incapacitated by laughter at its comedy. Bear in mind the Cubist's multiple views of his subject—but see them clearly, please, and neatly, not all jumbled up together.

2

The Game of the Name

SO different, one from the other, are the three faces of the computer that they may at first sight seem to be irreconcilable. But underlying them all, like the bone structure of a face seen from different sides, is a common base, though it takes some digging to find it.

I never meant to make a career out of finding that common element, and to the extent that it happened, I guess curiosity was responsible. My interest in computers was first aroused in 1950 by Mrs. Brauer, a knowledgeable and dedicated instructor who struggled gallantly to explain calculus to a bunch of engineers whose interest in the subject was less than intense.

She wasn't trying to arouse anyone's curiosity at the time. She was giving the class hell, as a matter of fact. "Why do you have to learn all this abstract theory? I'll tell you why, you dolts. Because without it you'll be unequipped to do anything remotely resembling mathematics. There are machines being built now to take care of the mechanics of computation, and they'll be a lot better at it than a band of trained monkeys masquerading as engineers. I intend to teach you to think mathematically, not to compete with machines in repetitive calculation. Now let's get back to the definition of differentiability. It will be on the final exam, I assure you."

She returned to her maze of deltas and epsilons, taking most of the class with her, but I stayed behind to chew on what she had said. "Machines to work out this kind of equation? Impossible. How in the world could they do it? Those machines would have to work like the human mind, and that can't be. I've got to find out what's going on."

It's tempting to identify that point as the beginning of an unswerving course to an exemplary career in computers. In reality, the path to a less than exemplary career in computers was marked by a series of random happenings, which, against the background of Mrs. Brauer's lively little lecture, became tentative steps toward satisfying my curiosity about how machines could solve mathematical equations. Finally the day came when I could say, "Aha! so that's how it's done."

But curiosity, it seems, is not that easily satisfied. The original question, "How do the machines work?" was promptly replaced by the desire to know what all the fuss was about. Why should there be any more confusion about computers than there is about tractors or sewing machines? Why couldn't everybody understand that what computers do is as mechanical as pulling a plow or poking a needle through fabric?

Slowly the suspicion has grown that the problem stems from a lack of awareness of the computer as a logic machine. The complexity of the finished product masks the basics to such a degree as to obscure totally the fact that its logical structure is what shapes it and what explains its seemingly divergent faces.

To add to the confusion, logic itself is poorly understood. If we're uncertain about what logic does for us, we must inevitably be uncertain about what the computer can do for us. Indeed, bestowing upon the computer the title of logic machine may enhance its undeserved reputation in relation to people unless we take remedial action to clarify exactly what logic is.

This is best done by taking a glance at history. The close kinship between logic and the computer cannot be understood without at least a rough sketch of the way the one grew into the other.

It all started, as so many things did, with the ancient Greeks, specifically with the great philosopher, Aristotle, in the fourth century B.C. In the case of logic, what Aristotle did was to discover that this particular way of thinking could be described by a set of rules and to list those rules. He was not the first human to use logical thinking, but he was the first to find that the rules could be written down and that they could be used to sort out thoughts as being or not being good logic.

When Aristotle's logic was rediscovered by Europeans many centuries after his death, it became little more than a source of fun and games for the cognoscenti. It was an intellectual playground for philosophers, theologians, teachers, and anybody else who had the time and inclination to join in the fun. A lot of books were written in which scholars explained things to each other, proved and disproved each other's theorems, and generally enjoyed themselves immensely. For centuries it remained basically static and barren, an academic exercise with an increasingly bad reputation among more practical men.

All that changed in 1854 when a man named George Boole published a book called *The Laws of Thought*, in which he demonstrated that Aristotle's logic system could be converted to a variation of simple algebra. He showed that even the most complicated logical relationships could be reduced to equations which could then be manipulated by simple mathematical operations.

Boole's work was of long-term significance in two major ways. It was the cause of a great furor among mathematicians and logicians, which is discussed in Chapter 8, but more relevant here is the fact that his off-beat algebra was an important ingredient in the history of the computer. When his novel approach to logic was mated with much later electronic technology, the computer was born.

But rather than retracing all the steps from Aristotle to Boole to the computer, we can make the great leap and directly link the origins of logic to the computer. With superbly honed hindsight we can cut across the centuries and make easily obvious something that was not obvious at all until somebody thought of it.

Of all the original work on logic that Aristotle and his followers did, two discoveries are immediately relevant to the computer. The first, and most basic, was the rule that you can deal logically only with things which you can absolutely divide into two categories. You must restrict yourself to statements about which it can be said yes or no, they are this or not this, they are true or false. But they must be one or the other.

The second major discovery was called the syllogism, which is nothing more than an orderly way of setting down a series of statements to establish whether or not the conclusion meets the requirements of good logic. There were several kinds of syllogisms, but we'll restrict ourselves to those that look like this:

1. All engineers are brilliant.
2. Caliban is an engineer.
3. Therefore Caliban is brilliant.

In a somewhat simplified vocabulary, you can call statements 1 and 2 the assumptions or premises, and statement 3 the conclusion. For this particular type of case, the ancient rule states that if the two premises are true, you are entitled to say that the conclusion is true. That kind of rule is a bit vague for modern tastes. It needs to cover all the possibilities more precisely. So change it to say that only if both premises are true will the conclusion be true; under all other conditions it will be false. Don't concern yourself with the possibility that Caliban may be brilliant without being an engineer. Remember that we're dealing with logic, not common sense.

Now, armed with those two simple rules from the golden age of Greece, take one giant step forward twenty-four centuries to the age of hobbies and build yourself a machine to handle syllogisms of that form automatically. You will need only a few parts, which you can find in any hardware store: one source of electricity, one light bulb, and two switches. Any ordinary switch will do, as long as it meets the basic requirements for use in a logic machine; it must have only two possible states (on or off) and it must always be in one or the other of those states. A switch like the one on your living room wall will do just fine.

(A word of caution. If you do actually build this gadget, better use a flashlight bulb, with batteries as your electricity source, rather than play around with the potentially lethal voltage in your house. The study of logic is a worthwhile pursuit but hardly one that you want to get killed for.)

As shown in the diagram, wire the ingredients so that the light goes on only when both switches are in the up position. If either switch is down, the light should be off. That's all there is to it. What you have made may look to you merely like a light that goes on when both of the two switches are up, but it really is a logic machine, a simple one, but still an honest-to-goodness device that can simulate the process of pure logic.

You accomplish the transformation from simple electrical circuit to logic device by playing the game of the name. While the name of this game may be new to you, the game itself is a very ancient one, derived from the primitive idea that there is magic in names. In some societies people kept their real names as closely guarded secrets and used phony names in public. They believed that if you let your real name be known to someone else, you could be in serious trouble. He who controlled your name could control you.

We moderns know that such ideas are pure nonsense. To us a name is only an arbitrary combination of sounds or symbols assigned as the identifier of some person or object. That's all names are, just symbols; there is no magic in them.

Nevertheless, names still seem to have a strange kind of power. By controlling the names of the pieces of our circuit, we will transmute a few hardware-store items into abstractions that belong in a college course.

To work the spell, you don't need any exotic ingredients or magic charms. Just find a pencil and some adhesive labels. The two switches you will call respectively, "Premise 1" and "Premise 2." The light bulb is dubbed "Conclusion." Those

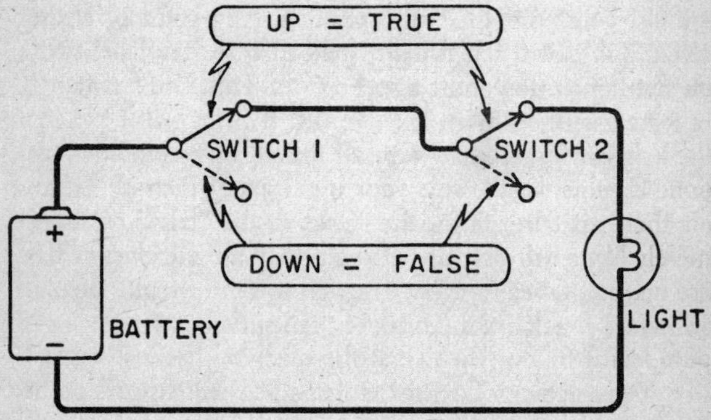

A HOMEMADE LOGIC MACHINE

parts now correspond to the three statements of the syllogism. Next you need names for the two positions of the switches, corresponding to the conditions of the two premises. Call the up position of each switch "true," and the down position "false." Finally, put a label beside the light bulb, reading: "Conclusion is true only if the light is on."

(If you don't feel qualified to build your own version of this gadget, you can still play the game. The people who built your car have been kind enough to wire it with all the essentials. The car radio will come on only when both the ignition switch and the radio switch are turned on. Call those two switches "Premise 1" and "Premise 2" and label the radio as "Conclusion." If the radio comes on, the conclusion is true.)

Now you're ready to work the machine. Use the syllogism about Caliban as a test, just to get the feel of it. Premise 1 was that all engineers are brilliant. You accept this as true, so you throw the switch called Premise 1 up, to the "true" position. Premise 2 was that Caliban is an engineer, which you likewise accept as true, so the switch called Premise 2 also goes up to the "true" position. Now you look at the light and discover that it is lit, indicating, as the label says, that the conclusion must also be true. This result matches the logic correctly.

You can experiment with all the possible combinations of the statements. Change your mind about Premise 1, decide that it is false, throw the switch to the "false" position, and the light will go out, showing that the conclusion has now become false. In every case you try, the circuit's behavior correctly matches the rules of the logic.

Does it follow, then, that the machine has just worked out an Aristotelian syllogism? Not at all. The light goes on or off because you wired it to respond to the switches in a certain way. The important thing we have done is to interpret the conditions of the circuit in such a way that they correspond to a set of logic rules. And that is the real key to computer design. The circuits have absolutely no ability to do logical thinking or any other kind of thinking. They simply handle electrical signals in accordance with the way they are wired. Nor is there any truth or falseness in electronic circuits. You could just as well call the two conditions red and blue, real and imaginary, Homer and Jethro; the names are completely arbitrary. But even though there is nothing more or less true about an open switch than about a closed one, by giving the right things the right names we can do a remarkably good job of duplicating logical processes.

Many devices are suitable for this kind of application: a switch being closed or open, a magnetic field being present or absent, a hole being punched or not punched in a card or a paper tape—there are any number that can do the job. The only requirement is that the device permit just two conditions to be possible, with all others excluded.

Inside the computer there are no simple electrical switches; there the logic functions are performed by the proper combination of electronic components. These "switching circuits," as they are called, will react to the proper electrical signals, the inputs, in much the same manner as those switches react to your fingers.

Instead of using the state of a labeled switch as the activator of the logic, most computers play the game of the name with two voltages, and the circuits are so designed that these are the only voltages that ever appear in the machine. For example, +5 volts and 0 volts might be used, with one of them being called true and the other false. Computer designers can become highly excited arguing over which name to give to which voltage, but I doubt if you share their sense of the dramatic. Neither do the circuits, which work exactly the same, regardless of how the names are assigned. To avoid arguments, most engineers who work on the viscera of the machine call the higher voltage "high" and the lower voltage "low," which may be unimaginative but works fine.

There is one more move to make with the gadget you built. We have given formal names to the switches and their positions, and to the light, but the gadget itself needs an appropriately dignified name, one that will relate it to the world of logic. A suitable one is to be found in your basic vocabulary. Like the man who was astonished to learn that he had been speaking prose all his life, you may not be aware that you have been using, since you were a child, three little words that are the essential language of Boolean algebra. Considering the vital role these words played in the development of the computer, you would have to classify them as among the most important few syllables in the world, and yet they are among the simplest: and; or; not.

Start with the normal meaning of "and," as in "It is hot and cloudy today." That total statement is true only when both parts of it are true. The labels on your machine say basically the same thing, reflecting the fact that the light will go on only when switch 1 *and* switch 2 are up. You can legitimately call your gadget an AND circuit. In computer jargon, you have mechanized the logical AND function. The OR and the NOT can be done just as easily. For example, your car has been wired so that the dome light will go on if one door switch *or* the other *or* the dashboard switch is closed. That is an OR circuit. To see the NOT operation in action, change the label on one of your gadget's switches, so it reads "false" instead of "true" when it is in the up position.

You have now duplicated all the circuits in a computer, except for memory, which I discuss in chapter 3. That's all there is inside the machine—just circuits to do those three things and combinations of them. In a time when everything seems to get ever more complicated, it may not seem possible that computer circuits are really so simple, but it's true.

And, or, not—three basic logic functions so elementary that you are rarely even aware of using them. Yet those three little operations are the building blocks from which any mathematical or logical structure is built. If you find it difficult to believe that such tasks as calculating a trajectory to Mars, designing an automobile's suspension system, or finding out whether a person has ever been arrested can be reduced to those simple steps, please don't argue. Proving this proposition was what caused George Boole to have a special kind of algebra named after him. It is the basis on which computers operate. Except for problems so fantastically complicated that even their great speed is inadequate, computers can do absolutely anything that can be expressed as a combination of those rudimentary operations.

In order to put Boole's ideas into practice, you must recognize that the circuits in a real computer, unlike your model, aren't used to make ordinary light bulbs go on and off. Instead, each circuit's output is used to drive other, similar circuits. By carefully controlling the conditions under which each signal assumes the condition called "true," or "high," you can activate different parts of the machine at your discretion, steer data around as you desire, and generally control what is happening under any particular set of conditions.

To accomplish this goal, computer designers don't deal with such statements as "Caliban is an engineer." They use the voltages to represent such conditions as "If the instruction code is Multiply *and* the multiplier digit is *not* zero *and* there are no error conditions, then activate the circuit that sends the multiplicand to the adder."

If you're interested in learning, in detail, how any particular computer operates, you'll have to cope with thousands of such elements. A computer is nothing but an endless collection of such detailed logic combinations, all of which must be correct before the machine will work properly. It is only because there are so many circuits in a computer that the final result is an awesomely complex machine, one whose basic nature is easily obscured. But despite the intricacy of the finished product, its working circuits remain close kin to the little machine you built.

Their kinship also extends to their limitations, to the things they can't do. So pick up your little logic machine to learn the final valuable lesson it can teach you about the computer. If you don't know or can't decide whether a statement is true or false and so are uncertain which way to throw one of the switches, you're on your own. The little machine will just sit there looking back at you until you make up your mind. It won't become impatient with your indecision, it won't offer any friendly suggestions, and above all it won't whisper the answer in your ear.

While that observation may seem perfectly obvious and pointless, it provides an important insight into the intellectual capability of a computer's logic. To prove it to yourself, take your AND circuit, and try this example on it.

1. All sexually permissive societies are decadent.
2. The U.S.A. is sexually permissive.
3. Therefore the U.S.A. is decadent.

Work the machine exactly as before, throwing switches 1 and 2 up if you believe the corresponding premises are true. If the light goes on when you are finished, then you have proved by logic that the United States is a decadent nation. You could even call a press conference and announce that you have used computer technology to verify the decadence of American society.

Now let your neighbor work the machine. If the light stays off when he is finished, he has used computer technology to prove that the United States is not decadent (at least for this reason). Which one of you is logically correct? You both are. Which one of you is right? Sorry, I never get involved in disputes between neighbors.

The point of the test is obvious: how can you expect so simple a machine to contribute anything of value to a subject as broad as the moral condition of an entire nation? Or to any other subject you care to choose? Clearly it is the person setting the switches who determines whether the light will be on or off; the machine simply reacts. For all it knows, it's still finding out whether Caliban is brilliant. It has no idea what the topic under discussion is, all it "knows" is which way you decide to throw the switches. Make your decision intelligently or stupidly, capriciously or seriously, with malice or benevolence, it doesn't matter. Whenever you say that two statements are true and flip the switches up, the light will go on.

The computer is larger, faster, and infinitely more complicated than your little machine, but it too must sit inertly until you decide which way its switches are to be set. It has as much knowledge as your gadget has of the subject under consideration; it is no more helpful when you are puzzled.

And there you have the basic elements of the computer. When joined together in their thousands they form the logical structure that is the skeleton underlying all the workings of the machine. They explain its power and its limitations. They are the reality behind all the mythology that has grown up around it and that must be clarified before the logic machine can be understood.

3

Remembrance of Things Fast

ONE of the most exasperating of the minor problems that technical people face is deciding what to call the new things they develop. They obviously have only two choices: they can create a new word, or they can use an old one. But simply as the alternatives may sound, scientists always get into trouble, no matter which one they choose.

If they make up new words like cybernetics or laser or firmware, they are accused of creating a jargon that gets them out of touch with the layman. "You must learn," they are told, "to communicate with the rest of us in language we can understand." But if they follow the other route and use an existing word, an equally undesirable hazard crops up. None of the available old words can be more than partly correct for describing the new thing. This partial accuracy leads people to the dangerous belief that they understand something when they really don't.

The situation is further complicated by the natural human tendency to anthropomorphize. Attributing human characteristics to nonhuman entities is not an uncommon custom. Pieces of pipe are called elbows and nipples; electrical connectors are designated as male or female; an automobile contains wrist pins and knuckle joints. But when this tendency is superimposed on the use of an old word in a totally new context, all sorts of problems are created.

The hazard exists in many fields of technology, but rarely are the problems so spectacular as they are with computers. Much computer mythology has its origins in the words that were chosen to describe the various parts and functions of the machine—for example, "decision" and "instruction." These terms mean almost the same thing in computers as they do in our ordinary conversation, but not quite, and it is the "not quite" that leads to confusion.

Consider the word "memory." Here is a word that went along happily for centuries, bouncing from one language to another and being no more and no less misunderstood than any other word in people's vocabularies. Everybody knew that memory was a faculty shared by people and certain other creatures, but always restricted to living things.

But as science moved ever forward it encountered a new kind of phenomenon that needed a name. There proved to be cases in the inanimate world where a characteristic from a past time was carried over to a later time. For lack of a better word, people chose to describe this property as "having memory." I first met this use of the word in an engineering course on materials. Certain metals, plastics, and other materials, I was told, tend to go back to a previous shape after they have been formed into a second shape. Metallurgists used to call this "memory," and maybe they still do.

Then, during the development of computers, a new problem came up that led to still another use of the old word. In many cases the basic logic circuits would produce a sequence of very short electrical pulses representing data which, for various reasons, could not be put to immediate use but which would be needed later. In order not to lose the information, a mechanism was needed to which the pulses could be sent for safekeeping before they disappeared. So the designers built something to which they could say, if you'll pardon the anthropomorphism, "Hold this for me, will you? There's a good lad. I'll be back to pick it up again in a little while."

In the early days of computers, this device was given different names on the two sides of the Atlantic. The British called it the storage or store, which is a good name because it's neutral and less subject to misunderstanding. In the United States it was usually called the memory. I always preferred the British term, but that battle was lost many years ago. Memory is the name that stuck and so it is the one I'll use.

This usage, however, implies that something in the machine corresponds to something with the same name in the human mind, an implication which has led to one of the most widespread misapprehensions about computers and is the origin of the first of the myths we need to examine. While the memory is a vitally important part of the computer itself, it is not equally important to the purpose of this book. But since it is the source of so much potential misunderstanding it should be disposed of early so that it doesn't keep getting in our way as we go about our business of clarifying the computer.

The distinction between the way people remember and the way the machine remembers is perfectly clear to those who work closely with computers, and especially to the engineers who design the memories. I don't know how you may visualize these designers, possibly as some kind of medical researchers. In reality they are electrical engineers who know about such specialized subjects as magnetic domains, addressing matrices, and the noise immunity of solid-state circuits. By no means are they experts at remembering, either; in fact their own memories often tend to fall considerably below the national average.

One of the best memory engineers we had in the early days of our group was Joe. We all looked to him on questions of how to optimize a differential amplifier, how to time a disturb pulse, how to select the best switching diodes. When it came to computer memories, he was a wizard.

One day he was given a different kind of assignment. "Joe," his boss told him, "I want you to go to lunch with two visitors today. They're from ILIC, the Incredibly Large Insurance Company, and they're thinking seriously about buying an incredibly large number of our computers. One of the things we have to show them is that we've got technical competence. So have lunch with them and talk memories." Joe was reluctant, but he went.

Everything was fine at first. The lively chatter ranged over current switches, the merits of word addressing, and the problems of lithium-ferrite cores. Joe was happy; the customers were impressed with the range and depth of his knowledge. But between the main course and the dessert, Joe excused himself to go to the washroom. When he came out, he stopped abruptly and looked around in momentary bewilderment, as though he had forgotten where the table was, which indeed he had. But his confusion lasted only a few seconds. He spotted his target, smiled, and headed back into the dining room. Moving with quiet confidence, he sat down and picked up the conversation about memories with two total strangers at the table next to the one he had left. ILIC never did buy any of our computers.

There really is no mystery about what a computer memory is. It is a device that receives a short pulse of electrical energy and undergoes a change that remains after the pulse has gone; it also provides some way to let us detect the change at a later time and so reconstruct the fact that it got the short pulse some time before. But that definition, although accurate, needs some amplification.

If you want a familiar parallel to the way a computer memory works, direct your attention, once again, to the switch on the wall of your room. Walk over to it, flip it up to turn the light on, and step away from it. You should, at this point, notice that after you take your hand away from the switch, it stays up and the light stays on. The switch remembers which way you flipped it.

If you're skeptical, walk back to it and push it down to turn the light off. You will notice that this time the switch stays down and the light stays off. Its memory works in both directions, up and down. If you object to the use of "remembers" and "memory" in this context, keep in mind that it is the usage employed for computers. Familiar old words are being applied in unfamiliar new contexts.

A technical point is in order here. The switches used for logic and those used for memory are not totally interchangeable. The memory switches must be the type that stay put after you flip them. Those used for logic can be the type that you have to hold for as long as you want them to be active. The analogous electronic circuits are designed in just that way, with the logic circuits activated only so long as the input pulses are present.

At any rate, the wall switch meets the first part of our definition of computer memory. You gave it a pulse of energy, and something inside changed and stayed changed after the pulse was gone. As you have probably anticipated, the time has come to play the game of the name once again, to use some of the magic that names aren't supposed to have, and change a simple piece of hardware into a component of the mysterious computer.

As before, the names we pick are completely arbitrary and in theory we have our choice of any words in the entire human lexicon. But in practice we'll call the up position of the switch the digit "1" and the down position the digit "0."

The only reason for the choice is that it's useful. Elements in the memory are generally thought of as handling data, rather than as performing logic functions, and the digits 1 and 0 make more sense for data.

Having gone that far, we can make one more move in the game and give the switch itself a new name. We'll call it "a memory element capable of storing one bit of information." Because the switch can remember the direction of the last pulse it got, it has met the first part of the definition. But to qualify completely as a memory, it will have to provide us with a way to determine at a later time what the state of the switch is and so to reconstruct the direction of the last pulse. There are two ways you can do this. The obvious one is to look at the light. If it is on, then the last pulse the switch got was in the up direction or, to put it in terms of the game, a 1 was stored in the memory element. If the light is off, a 0 was stored.

But what if the light bulb is burned out, or if it can't be seen from the switch? You can still very easily determine the switch's previous state. Just push up on it. If you feel it move or hear a click, it must have been down, so a 0 was stored. If it doesn't move, then it was already up, which means that a 1 was stored.

As simple as those two techniques may sound, they are fairly accurate analogies for the way information is retrieved from a computer's memory. The switch has met all the stated criteria for use as a memory element in a computer.

Despite the fact that ordinary switches would serve the purpose, memory elements in a computer are not made on the same principle as wall switches, any more than their logic counterparts are. There are no mechanical devices whatsoever that can function at the incredible speed that computers are designed for. The wall switch takes about half a second to change from one state to the other; modern computer memories are routinely expected to be able to operate about 500,000 times faster than that.

Computer memories are completely electronic, of course, and a surprising number of different gadgets have been found to do the job, all having the characteristic that a short electrical impulse will change the condition of the device and that this change will remain after the pulse has gone away.

The one most used for many years is the ferrite-core memory. It is made up of tiny doughnuts of magnetic material strung on a mesh of very fine wires. Down these wires go the electrical pulses in such a way that they magnetize the little rings in one of two directions. The names 1 and 0 are given to the two directions in which the little doughnuts can be magnetized. There are ways in which you can sense later the direction in which the magnetizing had been done and so can tell whether a 1 or a 0 was stored in the memory element.

Another popular type of memory element is made by interconnecting two transistors—it used to be vacuum tubes—in such a way that either one or the other is conducting current, depending on which of them last got a pulse; this hookup is called a "flip-flop." Here again, the names 1 and 0 are given to the two states of the device, and a way is provided for finding out later what the state is.

The ferrite core and the flip-flop (in a very tiny form) are by far the most common, but many other techniques have been used and more are being developed all the time. In some, exotic compounds are submerged in liquid hydrogen. Others consist of magnetic material in a wide variety of shapes and forms. The units used to store the massive amounts of information needed for large files and data banks are somewhat different. They usually have a magnetizable surface applied to a reel of plastic tape or a set of large metal disks. On these surfaces the 1s and 0s are recorded as little magnetized or not-magnetized spots. They are similar in operation to a tape recorder and are no more deserving of the name "memory."

By now you're probably wondering whether all this has anything whatever to do with memory, even in the very restricted sense that we've defined it. All we have so far is a gadget—mechanical, magnetic, electronic, whatever—which can be flipped at will between its two possible states. To use these gadgets to store useful information, we have to take a few more steps.

Instead of thinking about only one of those elements, take several of them and treat them as a group. In the official, authorized version of the computer lexicon, such a group is called a "byte." I have no idea where the word came from, and I agree that it's an ugly little word. In fact, I dislike it so much that I won't use it; from here on those groups of elements will be called just plain "groups."

Picking the number of elements that should be used to make up a group is one of the most basic decisions in the design of a computer, because much of the machine's detailed structure follows from that choice. As a result it is always the cause of lively debate among computer designers. Whatever the choice, each single element within the group is still capable of representing only a 0 or a 1. But the number of possible combinations of these simple choices gets quite large when you work with groups of them. Six elements, for example, can form 64 possible combinations, from all 0s to all 1s. If you give a meaning to each of these combinations, then 64 different meanings can be assigned to a group of 6 elements. Those 64 meanings are enough to cover the mundane information with which a computer is concerned. You can "code" the alphabet, the digits from 0 to 9, + and − signs, special symbols, all sorts of things. You have given the computer its vocabulary.

Now that the elements have been organized into groups

capable of conveying information, the next step is to put together many thousands of these groups into a single package. You then provide a way of steering the pulses to or from any particular group, and you have a system formally called "a binary digital memory."

Which brings us to the question we're really concerned with: what resemblance such a system bears to the human memory. Although nobody knows how people's memories work, there are enough obvious differences to make it clear that any comparison between man's memory and the machine's is little more than a quaint parable.

Certainly the most fundamental difference between the two kinds of memory is in the filing system, the way in which the information that has been stored is located and brought out at a later time. In a computer, once you have wired all the groups of elements together, you have defined a location for each of them. From that point on, all the information is identified solely by its location in the wired-up system, like apartments in a building or boxes in a post office. In fact, official computer jargon refers to these locations as "addresses."

All information in a computer memory is handled in terms of its address, with no concern for what the contents may be. It's like doing business with people whom you never see but whose address you know. The only way you can refer to them is as "Occupants, Apartment 17C." It doesn't matter whether their name is Smythe or Pilbund, whether they are pleasant or grouchy, young or old, quiet or noisy—we know nothing but their address. And when they move out of their apartment and others move in, the new people, whoever they may be, become the occupants of apartment 17C and nothing changes. That's how computer memories work. They find information only by its location in the system.

On the other hand, how the living memory runs its filing system is a complete mystery. How we store things away and how we find them again seem only loosely tied to the location of the information; in fact we're not even sure that there are specific locations in which specific items are stored. Our retrieval system seems to be geared, rather, around the contents of our memories. We know what's in there, but not where it is. We know the Smythes and the Pilbunds. We know whether they are pleasant or grouchy, young or old, quiet or noisy. The only thing we don't know is which apartment they occupy.

The difference was recognized very early in the development of computers, and there has been intermittent work at trying to make the machine's memory work more like people's do. The goal has proved very elusive, and opinions vary as to whether any progress has been made toward it. Some researchers feel that the theoretical solution already exists and that only practical problems stand in the way—such as the vast number of elements required and the fantastic cost of building a working model. But most computer people are skeptical, because there are other differences beside the nature of the filing systems.

Take, for example, the question of selectivity. In the sense that a computer remembers, all computers remember everything equally well. Any pattern of 1s and 0s gets stored with indiscriminate efficiency, with no preference for any particular kind of data. But in the sense that people remember, there is favoritism and bias and arbitrariness.

I have read some speculation that people never really lose a memory, that we store forever every sensation and event we have ever experienced. That may be true, but somehow we are unable to find some of those things when we want them. We all have our own individual variations of this selectivity. In my own case, I have a terrible time remembering faces, prices, and colors, but no difficulty recalling geography, history, and things people say to me. I find it impossible to remember memory aids, even the most common ones like "Thirty days hath September," but I can remember every detail of the first digital circuits I worked with more than twenty years ago. Such quirks are neither typical nor unusual. Almost everybody remembers some things poorly and some things well.

It's as though we had in our heads some kind of desk clerk who looks at all incoming applicants and assigns them to rooms. The ones he is interested in or enjoys or really wants to remember get good rooms right off the lobby, where they can be found with no trouble and revisited often and easily. The others get sent to dingy cells in distant corners of the basement, where they gather dust and cobwebs and find their way out with difficulty, if they ever get out at all. There is absolutely nothing in a computer that even remotely corresponds to this selectivity. Binary digital systems don't behave that way.

A point that seems to be related is the role of repetition in remembering. With the switchlike elements of a computer memory, a pattern of 1s and 0s is always stored on the first try. It is always retrieved correctly, regardless of what the pattern is. If it isn't, then something needs fixing. Repetition won't help. With people, repetition not only helps, it is sometimes vital. Nobody ever learned the multiplication tables, or "to be or not to be," or even a telephone number without painful repetition. It's as though being persistent with the desk clerk gets the information a better room in Memory Hotel.

There is no need to try to list all the unknowns and all the puzzles of human memory. It is enough simply to point out the incredible assumption required to accept the idea that there is any similarity between the two systems. You would have to believe that all the things we remember—colors, sounds, smells, shapes, rhythms, textures, sensations, faces—are converted by the mind into a set of 1s and 0s and stored away in that form. I can't visualize anyone's taking the idea seriously.

Can you imagine the result if a competent memory engineer like Joe were to analyze the human memory? He would certainly react like a meticulous file clerk looking around a typical attic. "How can you find what you're looking for? Why are you keeping all that old junk in the corner? Nothing is labeled, nothing is in order. What a bloody mess!" And even if he were to concede that, by some miracle, such a slipshod mechanism might be able to function, he would surely deny the possibility that any kind of intelligence could be designed around it.

But somehow the human memory works. And it works so differently from a binary digital memory with its totally location-dependent functioning, its restriction to combinations of 1s and 0s, that you have to conclude that one or the other has been given the wrong name.

4

Answers and Questions

EVERY day of our lives we face problems. They range from tiny to overwhelming, from completely routine to totally unexpected. They follow one another as relentlessly as the games of the baseball season. Some people thrive on them, some people break under them, but everybody has real problems that need solving.

The computer, they tell us, can solve problems, so it would seem only natural to turn to it for help. Not for anything exotic, mind you; you don't need a flight plan to the moon, you're not interested in drowning yourself in an ocean of paper, you're not compiling a dossier on your neighbors. But surely that electronic wonder can do something to help us ordinary folk with the kind of real problems we all face all the time? Any one of us could make a list of them: How much allowance should our fifteen-year-old boy get? Should we sell the house and move into an apartment? How many rolls of wallpaper would it take to do the living room? Is this a good time to trade in the old car? How much insurance should we be carrying? Will I bother to vote in the next election?

Every question on the list would make a good starting point for an examination of the second myth about computers. Suppose we pick at random (a carefully selected random) the one about wallpaper. Now assume the role of an average house dweller who wants new wallpaper in the living room but doesn't remember how to calculate the number of rolls he will need. You go to your local computer company and say that you have a problem you would like the machine to solve. You are told that only authorized personnel may approach the computer, but would you like to talk to one of our programmers? Sure, why not? You follow directions and find the door labeled ASK ME ANYTHING. You enter, and there, smiling paternally, sits the programmer.

"How much wallpaper will I need to do my living room?" you ask.

"No problem. I know how to figure that out," he says happily. "Wallpaper is sold by the roll, so we have to find the area of the surface to be covered and divide by the area of a roll of wallpaper. That will give us the number of rolls we'll need. Tell me, how big is your living room?"

"About average size."

"I'm sorry," he replies, "but that is insufficiently precise. The computer must have the exact dimensions before it can solve your problem."

You go back home, measure the room, and return with the information that it is 14 feet long, 12 feet wide, and 8 feet high.

"Your room has four walls, a floor, and a ceiling. Which of them do you want covered?"

"Just the walls. The floor is carpeted and the ceiling is mirrored."

"Are there any doors or windows?"

"Of course there are doors and windows. But let's forget about them. They aren't very big and, besides, I'm too tired to go all the way home and back here again."

You still haven't satisfied the programmer. His next

question is, "Do you know how much wallpaper there is in a roll?"

You phone a store and find that there are single and double rolls—which did you want? For a brief moment you consider switching to paint, but you decide on single rolls, each of which, you are told, is 30 feet long and 24 inches wide. This information you report to the programmer.

He jots down all the numbers and checks them with you. He mutters something about ANS Cobol in middle-ground mode under DDOS in a TS environment and disappears through a door marked COMPUTER ROOM. KEEP OUT. A short time later he reappears with a confident smile on his face.

"No problem," he reports. "You will need 0.5778 rolls. You can round it off to 1."

"Are you sure? That seems like a very small amount of wallpaper."

"You know, the same thought had occurred to me. It does seem a bit skimpy, doesn't it?"

The programmer pores over his print-out, mutters, checks things off with his pencil, and suddenly bangs his forehead with the palm of his hand.

"Damn it! I forgot to convert the width of the roll from inches to feet. That won't be any problem."

Again he disappears into the computer room and in due time emerges wearing a triumphant grin. "You'll need 6.933 rolls, but you can round it off to 7. Better buy 8."

Your problem has now been solved by the computer. Or so mythology would have us believe. Take a closer look.

If you had followed the programmer into the computer room, you would have found that the result of all the work he did was a series of "instructions" that were fed into the machine. At first glance these instructions look like a meaningless string of numbers. What they are, however, is a series of codes for activating the proper computer circuits in the proper sequence.

The official procedure at this point is to say that these instructions "tell the computer what to do in a language it can understand." Accept that description for the moment, even though it is vague and misleading, and try to put some meaning into it. To do that, transform yourself from the role of the homeowner to that of the computer, and see what the program looks like from its point of view. Since you don't understand the language that the computer understands, I have made myself your interpreter and put it into English.

If you're interested enough to try to follow the instructions, you need only know that the letters refer to portions of the computer's memory. If you're even more interested and have always wanted to play computer, then follow along. Take a piece of paper, write the letters A to H across the top, and do what the instructions say. When an old number is replaced by a new one, strike out the first and write in the second. You'll be doing exactly what the computer does.

Here's what the computer is instructed to do:

1. Put the following numbers in the respective memory locations: 14 in A, 12 in B, 8 in C, 30 in D, 24 in E, and 12 in F.

2. Add the number in A to the number in A. Put the result in H.

3. Add the number in B to the number in H. Put the result in H.

4. Add the number in B to the number in H. Put the result in H.

5. Multiply the number in C by the number in H. Put the result in H.

6. Multiply the number in D by the number in E. Put the result in G.

7. Divide the number in G by the number in F. Put the result in G.

8. Divide the number in H by the number in G. Put the result in G.

9. Print the number in G.

10. Stop. (A computer must be instructed to stop, just as an automobile must.)

That is what the computer program looks like when you translate it from numbers to words. That's what the computer is instructed to do in a language it can understand, and a couple of things about it are worth noting. First, it hardly makes for spine-tingling drama. You might, in fact, call it tedium's finest hour. Every problem that goes into a computer takes the form of a series of detailed steps like these. Each of the steps spells out exactly what is to happen inside the machine. Every step is carried out by the machine exactly as entered. There is no provision for novelty, imagination, or deviation from the prescribed course.

But the most significant thing about this program can be found by imagining that you are looking at it for the first time. Forget that you set out to paper a room. Erase from your mind the discussion with the programmer. Just look at the list of instructions the way the computer gets them, and try to figure out what is going on. All you have is a series of additions, multiplications, and divisions. Nothing about living rooms or rolls of wallpaper appears anywhere in the litany. Nowhere is there any reference to the subject at hand, and that is completely characteristic of computer programs. Trying to figure out what a program relates to, simply by looking at it, is an almost impossible task.

There is a sermon to be drawn from this simple lesson. It deals with the fact that when you start with a solution, it's generally not possible to reconstruct the problem. And whenever you look at a computer program you are looking, not at a problem, but at a solution. You don't put a question into the machine, you put in the answer. The computer, it seems, is the victim of a verbal mix-up.

The situation is not unusual, because the confusion between problems and solutions is epidemic in our society. Much of the population of the country seems to be running around peddling answers without making any effort to find out what the questions are. It makes for interesting debate and lots of excitement, some of it harmless, some of it not. In this case it has led to the creation of the second and most widespread of the myths about computers. You may be surprised to hear the "fact" that computers solve problems labeled a myth, but that's what it is. Computers don't solve problems, despite the fact that everybody says they do and behaves as though it were a well-established truth.

Think back for a moment over the solution to the wallpaper problem. The critical step was taken by the programmer when he identified the right process to use: to find the area to be covered, and to divide it by the area of a roll of paper. The rest of the dialogue involved only getting the right numbers to work with. The programmer then completed the job by breaking the solution into simple steps that match the functions the computer is wired to do.

But the important thing is that the solution was identified by the person, in this case the programmer. The solution, not the problem, was then fed into the machine. That's true of all problems of this nature. If you seek out that hypothetical programmer and ask him to design a television picture tube or a nuclear accelerator, to compute a payroll or the interest due on a bank account, to figure out the date of the next lunar eclipse or the best route for a delivery truck to follow, in every case he will take you through the same steps that were followed in figuring out how many rolls of wallpaper to buy. In every case the problem must first be solved, and then the solution is fed into the machine.

This limitation should not come as a great revelation. It is completely characteristic of machines. No one in a normal state of health and sobriety would walk up to a bulldozer and say, "Build me a highway from Ashtabula to Cuyahoga Falls." You have to do things like turning ignition keys, controlling tread speed, raising blade, lowering blade, shifting gears. And even before you do those things, you had better plan and design the highway, so that the "instructions" you give the machine are the right ones. Design a highway and the bulldozer can push the dirt around for you. Solve a problem and the computer can push the numbers around for you.

That is easy to see in the case of the wallpaper calculation. It's a trivial example, and you may wonder how valid it is: whether that kind of problem would ever actually be programmed to run on a computer. It certainly would not, if you only wanted to work out the solution once. A low cost, economy model computer would run through that little program in less than 100 microseconds (a microsecond is one millionth of a second), which means that before you could take your finger off the starter button the computer would be printing the answer. It's hardly an efficient way to use the machine, and certainly not worth all that discussion with the programmer.

But if you had to solve that trivial problem tens of thousands of times a day you might well use the machine. Many sensible computer applications don't need much more mathematics than our example did. It doesn't require much calculus to figure out the agent's commission on an insurance premium or the balance in an average bank account. But when you have to handle tens of thousands of insurance policies or bank accounts every day, a computer becomes immensely helpful. Again, it's like the bulldozer. Most people are quite capable of hoisting and moving a few shovelfuls of clay or sand, but when you want to move ten thousand times that much, a bulldozer comes in very handy.

At this point, though, there is one tremendous difference between the computer and the bulldozer. With an earth-moving machine, even when the work to be done is highly repetitive, the operator must always run the machine as though the actions had never been carried out before. To the earth-moving machine every pile of dirt is a brand-new situation.

The computer, on the other hand, does have its "memory," and the instructions can be stored in it as easily as can the data on which the instructions will work. So if you wanted to calculate the wallpaper problem ten thousand times a day, you would write the program in exactly the same way, except that step 10, instead of being "Stop," would be "Go to the place in the memory where step 1 has been stored." At step 1, new numbers could be brought in from punched cards or magnetic tape, and the computer would automatically crank out the results. The operator's job would consist solely of feeding the punched cards in the front end and hauling the printed paper away from the other.

If this program were to be used often, it would be permanently stored in the computer's magnetic tape or disk system. It would be retrieved from storage, when required, by the use of a code, usually in the form of a cute acronym. In this case, the program might be called ALLWET, standing for Approximate Linear Length of Wallpaper Estimating Task. An announcement would be duly made by the originator that the ALLWET program is now available, and it could be sold to or stolen by any number of other computer users. After it had gone through enough hands, its origins would be lost, the computer would be said to know how to calculate the amount of wallpaper required for any room, and the distinction between problems and solutions would have been blurred a little bit more.

At this point controversy arises, because many computer people take a different stand. "Hold on there," they say. "Is there any difference between the way the computer learned to solve the problem and the way the programmer learned the same thing? Didn't they both at some time have to be taught the steps of the solution, and didn't they both have to reach into their memories to apply that solution? If you call it problem solving when the human does it, then why not grant the machine the same courtesy?"

It's a good argument, and can only be answered by confessing that I have been guilty of using "problem" and "solve" as loosely as everyone else. By a more rigorous definition, the programmer didn't solve the wallpaper problem any more than the computer did.

What we have come up against is the impasse that most such discussions eventually reach—the matter of defining terms. When I say that neither the machine nor the programmer solved the problem, I am being pedantic but with good reason. A very fine distinction is needed to separate what the machine does from what people do.

This is an occasion when the trouble must be blamed on the poverty of the language. The word "problem" tries to cover too much territory and does not describe adequately the differences in concept that we need.

In order to fill the gap, and to separate in my own mind what the computer can do from what it can't, I find it helps to divide problems into two categories which, for lack of better names, I choose to call presolved problems and true problems.

The presolved kind are called that simply because someone has already done the hard part of the job. Almost all working applications of the machine, ranging from the most trivial to the most elaborate, are in this category. The procedure is the same whether you want to calculate the point of impact of a guided missile, the sales tax on a bottle of Scotch, the handicaps for the office bowling league, or the neutron flux in a nuclear reactor.

The problem is truly solved when someone identifies the factors that must be taken into account in the problem, and then determines their mathematical relationship to one another in the form of an equation or a procedure. For some problems, such as the wallpaper one, that was done centuries ago. It is the step the computer can never take.

Once the proper procedure is found, the answer for a specific case can be obtained by assigning numerical values to the factors and then breaking the whole procedure into simple steps. Now it can go into the computer. This is the phase at which you can argue that machine and person are doing the same thing, because here you are dealing with the solution, not the problem.

There is a subdivision of this kind of problem whose presolved nature is much less obvious. The reason for relegating these to the class of subdivision is that practically none of the programs for such problems lie in the main stream of practical computer applications. They are mostly written as part of the academic research into the limits of what the machine can do. They include such things as game playing, theorem proving, and puzzle solving.

The accomplishments are very real. Computers have indeed been programmed to become respectable opponents in a game of chess, to prove mathematical theorems, and to work out certain kinds of logic and number puzzles. All those things have been done and beyond any doubt the results will continue to be improved upon. The game of chess will be played better and better. The theorems that can be proved will grow more complex. The puzzles that can be worked out will become more difficult.

These problems have a set of characteristics that make them fit well into a logical system like the computer. For one thing, you always know what goal you are working toward. There is a statement at the very beginning which tells you exactly where you want to go. You are also given a set of rules which rigidly specify what kind of operations you are allowed to use in moving toward your goal. Naturally, to fit into the computer's world, those steps must be totally reducible to the "and," "or," "not" type of logic that its elements perform.

A theorem in mathematics, for example, starts with a statement of what you are trying to prove. You are given a goal and you must show that it can be reached from the data you are given, using only the steps that are permitted within the system. In games like chess the same general condition is also true. Again you have a specific goal to reach and specific rules that must be followed in getting there. All these are, theoretically at least, within the scope of what the computer can be programmed to do.

The category I've chosen to call the true problem is entirely different. It has no prestated conclusion. The rules to be followed may or may not be known, and it is often difficult, if not impossible, to figure out whether the solution finally arrived at is the best, or even if it is a good one. In brief, this kind of problem involves trying to figure out how to get where you want to go without knowing for sure where you want to go.

You can easily recognize this if you go back over the list of problems the average person might raise—problems about allowances for children, trading cars, and carrying insurance—and I may appear to have unfairly loaded the examples to favor my definition. But the same condition holds true in highly technical fields where the computers are available, the programming talent is on hand with pencils poised, and the problem, but not the solution, can be described in precise terms.

A few questions that I would describe as true problems in science are: Why do some tropical storms become hurricanes while others don't? Is there any way to design a supersonic airplane that won't make a boom? Is it possible to make a photographic film without silver and still keep all the fine features of the present films?

There are any number of such problems in the physical sciences. In none of them is the end result yet known. There is as yet neither a knowledge of what the critical factors are, nor an equation showing how they relate to one another, nor a way of giving them numerical values. In some cases there is not even any assurance that there is a solution. That is what I call a true problem. None of them can be solved by the computer, even if you include the programmer as part of the system.

If and when these problems are solved, it will be done by people. Somebody will get a bright idea, find a relationship between variables that hadn't been noticed before, discover an obscure research paper on a different subject, or maybe have a dream one night that opens the door to the solution.

Once our problem solver has come up with a glimmer of the answer, he can go to the computer for help. He can use it to manipulate massive equations; he can correlate mountains of experimental data; he can work out theoretical test cases; he can do all the "number crunching" he needs in order to study the implications of his ideas. He may even find in the computer's results a trend or an anomaly that gives him fresh ideas to modify his theory, or go back and try a different approach.

In this kind of interaction it's easy to lose the distinction between what the person is doing and what the machine is doing in the problem-solving effort. But confusion can be avoided if you keep in mind the difference between the question and the answer. You can either raise to my own high standards your discrimination between a problem and a solution, or, if such pedantry doesn't suit your life style, you can categorize problems into those that have already been solved and those that haven't. The computer can help with one, but not with the other.

By the way, remember that the computer, as a logic machine, can be made to do anything that can be done with pure logic. What we have, then, is a limitation in solving problems that applies not just to the computer, but to logic itself. This is important as we proceed to the third and last myth about the machine, the myth that it can make decisions.

5

Three Minus Four Equals Decision

AT first glance it is not obvious that doing arithmetic and making decisions have much in common. We learned the two skills under entirely different circumstances—one in the classroom, the other through our experiences in "the arena of life." There is no clear link between the two abilities, either. Someone who can do arithmetic well does not necessarily make good decisions, and vice versa. Finally, in arithmetic there is always one correct solution, which we can check and verify, but decisions can have several good alternative results or no bad ones. In general, we have learned to treat arithmetic and decision making as two neatly compartmented areas, independent and unrelated.

Despite all those differences, a review of arithmetic is the best path to the root of the myth that computers make decisions. This fable is heard a lot less frequently now than it used to be, and that's a good thing. On the other hand, the infrequency of the statement may be due to the belief that it is so well established as to need no repetition. It may have become one of those things that "everybody knows."

What everybody may not know is that the secret to making decisions with a computer is an odd way of subtracting. By the way, it's never called "decision making" among computer people. They call it "test and branch," or "jump," or "conditional transfer of control." By whatever name, things have worked out in a strange way. What looks like nothing more than a cute trick in arithmetic becomes one of the keys to the most versatile machines ever made.

Not only do we have to deal with arithmetic but we have to deal with it at its most basic level. It may sound like a contradiction, but while computers handle calculations of truly unbelievable complexity, they themselves operate with only the fundamentals—involving, not the calculus you learned in college or the algebra you learned in high school, but the arithmetic you learned in the early grades of elementary school. So furrow your brow and sharpen your pencil, because we are going to brush up on your second- or third-grade arithmetic, starting with a true story as an example of the kind of easy problems involved.

For about a year during my teens I worked in a shoe factory. Since I had, at that time, completed three years of high school, read books at lunch time, and wore glasses, the title of "the professor" was bestowed upon me. It became my duty to act as a court of appeals to which all disputes of an intellectual nature could be referred.

One day George and Steve broke in on my reverie as I sat hammering nails into an endless stream of heels and uppers.

"Listen, Professor," said George, "how much is nothing times seven?"

"Nothing times seven? That's nothing."

They both nodded agreement. "Now," said George, "how much is seven times nothing?"

"Seven times nothing is also nothing."

"See!" yelled George.

"Wrong!" yelled Steve.

I looked at Steve in amazement. "What do you mean 'wrong'? What else could the answer be?"

"Seven times nothing," he said, "is seven, and I can prove it."

And prove it he did. He reached back to a storage rack, took seven shoes, and put them on the bench. "What do you see there?"

"Seven shoes," was the only possible answer.

"Okay, now don't multiply them by anything and what do you have?"

None of my scholastic arguments could counter his practical demonstration, and he won his point. It wasn't until twelve years later, on a lonely midnight shift, struggling to get the computer to multiply properly, that the answer to the forgotten incident suddenly occurred to me. The multiplier tells you how many times to add the multiplicand. When Steve reached up 1 time to bring down 7 shoes, he was multiplying 7 by 1. He should have reached up 0 times. You learned that in school, but most likely forgot it, just as I did. It's an example of the kind of arithmetic computers make you re-learn.

Return with me now to that distant time when you were first initiated into the mysteries of subtraction. Your teacher probably used such visual aids as wooden blocks, apples, or a cardboard pie cut into pieces. You were instructed to count out a pile of, say, 6 of the pieces, take away 2, count how many remained, and be led to the discovery that 6 take away 2 leaves 4. It was an easy task, and you had very little trouble mastering the routine.

But one day the teacher made life difficult by giving you a problem where 6 had to be subtracted from 2. This obviously qualified as a stupid question, since you had not yet learned about negative numbers. Your teacher explained, however, that when the 6 and the 2 were parts of longer numbers, there was a way out. You were shown that you could turn the 2 into a 12 by "borrowing" a 1 from the next column, and the problem became trivial, as the mathematicians say.

That was a branch point in your mathematical career, because it was where the entire class split into two groups. One group understood what the teacher was doing and would be able to subtract in later life. The rest were completely bewildered and have never been able to cope with the mystery. I'm in the latter group; my understanding of the subject is entirely theoretical.

Your final step in learning subtraction was to memorize a table covering all possible combinations of wooden blocks, apples, or cardboard pie. With that committed to memory, you were qualified to go forth into the world and subtract. You had learned the technique that we all live with, more or less comfortably and more or less proficiently.

Now I'm going to ask you to forget temporarily what you learned and look at a different way of subtracting. I'm even going to change the names of the numbers involved. You learned them as minuend, subtrahend, and difference, but I never could remember which was which and got into the habit of calling them the top number, the bottom number, and the answer. I'm too old now to break that habit.

There are a number of variations of this way of subtracting, but they all have the same basic purpose: to convert subtraction into addition. It sounds like a dim-witted exercise, but there are a couple of very good reasons for taking such a roundabout path to what appears to be a simple problem. One of them has to do with those negative numbers that were such a mystery in the third grade.

If you were asked today what $2-6$ equals, you would quickly work out the answer to be -4. The way you do it is to look at the problem and observe that the bottom number is bigger than the top one. So you interchange them, and then make the answer negative to compensate for interchanging.

You do it by habit and don't give much thought to the fact that you're using the basic algebraic equality $(a-b)=-(b-a)$. It doesn't really matter whether or not you remember the reason, the important thing is that you decide how to proceed by looking at the numbers and noticing which is bigger.

A computer can't do that. The only way it can "tell" which of two numbers is bigger is by subtracting one from the other and determining whether the answer is positive or negative. So you're trapped. Using the old system, the computer can't subtract until it knows which number is bigger, but it can't determine that without subtracting. The way out of this dilemma proves to be changing subtraction into a strange kind of addition. This technique has another benefit. It means that a computer can get by with only one chunk of circuits to do arithmetic—an adder. Once an adding unit is built, the computer can do all four basic mathematical operations.

So you want to subtract, using only addition. To accomplish that noble goal, you must be introduced to one more idea about numbers, the 9's complement. Now, the 9's complement of a number is simply the difference between 9 and the number; the sum of a number and its 9's complement is 9. It's easiest to see the idea if you break all the digits into pairs; 0 and 9, 1 and 8, 2 and 7, 3 and 6, 4 and 5. In every pair, 9 minus one of the numbers gives you the other.

"Aha," you say, "but to find the 9's complement you have to subtract the number from 9." No. There are a number of ways in which the 9's complement can be found in a computer without subtracting. You'll have to take that on faith. Proving it would take you deeper into the subject than you would care to go at this time, and probably at any future time.

The way you use the 9's complement in this strange

subtraction is as follows: First, write the problem in the normal way, as if you were going to subtract in the manner to which you are accustomed. Second, rewrite it with the same top number, but with a new bottom number—the 9's complement of the original one. Third, add the two numbers together and see what happens.

An example shows that it's a lot easier than it sounds. Take the case of 97 – 68, and see if we get the right answer, 29. Write it first in the old familiar form:

```
       97
minus  68
       --
```

To do it the new way, the bottom number, 68, now has to be changed to its 9's complement. Do it digit by digit. The complement of 6 is 3, for 8 it's 1. So our new bottom number is 31. Now rewrite the problem as an addition using this bottom number, and it looks like this:

```
      97
plus  31 (the 9's complement of 68)
     ---
     128
```

Well, we expected to get 29 for the answer and didn't quite make it, though it's exactly the answer that most computers would give you at this point in the proceedings. Forget for the moment whether the answer is right or wrong. The important thing is that the answer has more digits than the other two numbers. A 1 appeared at the left, an unfailing indication that the top number of the original problem is bigger than the bottom one, that the answer is positive.

If you want the right numerical answer, just take the 1 that came off the end and add it to the rest of the answer. Work out okay? That's how the computer does it, too.

Nobody can become proficient in something so simple with only one example to go by. You'll keep looking for the part that's hard to understand, when there really isn't any. So try another one, like 60 − 1. Old style, you would write the problem like this:

$$\begin{array}{r} 60 \\ \text{minus } \underline{01} \end{array}$$

The reason for writing "01" instead of "1" is that, for this technique to work, both numbers must be the same length. That doesn't present any great problem, it simply means you have to write in front of the shorter number the zeros you usually leave out. With your newly acquired skills, you would now do it this way:

$$\begin{array}{r} 60 \\ \text{plus } \underline{98} \\ 158 \end{array} \text{ (the 9's complement of 01)}$$

Again, the 1 on the left end says that the answer is positive, and if you take the 1 around to add it to the rest of the answer, you get 59, the correct solution to 60 − 1.

Those examples show how the technique works when you get a positive result—that is, when the top number is bigger than the bottom one. Now look at what happens when the opposite is true. Take a pair of numbers, say 21 and 46, and subtract each one from the other, to compare what happens in each case. You should get the same answer both times, with one being positive, the other negative.

When you set up the two problems side by side, they look like this.

$$\begin{array}{r} 46 \\ \text{minus } \underline{21} \end{array} \qquad \begin{array}{r} 21 \\ \text{minus } \underline{46} \end{array}$$

The one on the right probably bothers you. Mentally you have already reversed the numbers to get the bigger one on top. But remember that a computer can't see which number is bigger. Furthermore, it doesn't rebel at following instructions that "don't look right." We proclaimed a set of rules to be followed, and that's precisely what it will do under all conditions. So proceed exactly as before with both cases. Take the 9's complement of the bottom number and add it to the top number, just as the instructions say, and see what happens.

46	21
plus 78	plus 53
124	074

You know how to convert the first one to a positive 25. The other one, however, seems to be beyond hope. It isn't even close to negative 25. For one thing, what's that 0 doing at the front of the answer? Well, since a 1 didn't show up there, and since we're dealing with the computer where everything must be either a 1 or a 0, we have to say that a 0 was there. And just as a 1 is interpreted as a positive answer, so the 0 is the indication of a negative answer, the sign that the top number of the problem is smaller than the bottom one. The strangeness of the numerical part of the answer, 74, is just as easily explained. If you take its 9's complement you get 25, which, in combination with the negative indicator, is the correct result.

Those are the two cases you have in this kind of subtraction: a 1 or a 0 appearing at the left end. The 1 gets translated into a plus sign for the answer, and you add the 1 back to the right end to get the correct number. The 0 becomes a minus sign and is your signal to take the 9's complement of the answer.

About now, the more mathematically inclined will be reaching for pencil and paper to try to find a case where the system doesn't work. Save your energy. The technique may look like something out of the puzzle page of a Sunday newspaper, but it is firmly based in mathematics. It works. It even works, with the necessary modifications, in different number systems, such as the binary or any other you care to use.

And about now, the less mathematically inclined will be feeling the advent of an anxiety attack, reminiscent of the day you learned that there was no escape from taking Algebra II next year. Relax. Unless you plan to make a career out of designing or servicing computers, there is no need to understand in any depth what's going on. I certainly don't recommend that you try to do your subtraction this new way. It's fine for computers but unacceptably cumbersome for people. All you have to remember is that there is a way of subtracting one number from another in which getting a 1 or a 0 at the left end indicates whether the answer is positive or negative.

Of course, calling the extra digit a 1 or a 0 is just another aspect of the game of the name. Inside the computer, that digit really takes the form of a wire connected to one of the basic circuits in the adding unit. The voltage on that wire has two possible states. When it is in one of them, we call it a 1; when it's in the other, we call it a 0. If the wire is properly connected to other AND's, OR's, and NOT's, the state of its voltage can affect the course of events inside the machine. Depending on whether that voltage is high or low, the circuits it activates will cause the computer either to continue in the normal sequence of instructions or to go to the place in the memory where another set of instructions is stored—in effect, to switch the computer from one program to another.

And that's how the computer makes decisions.

At this point the going gets rather touchy. On the one hand, it's easy to speak in general terms about the remarkable power of this simple trick, making such sweeping statements as "This capability is so basic as to be an ingredient any machine must have if it is to be called a computer" or "No computer program of any significance can be written without the use of this decision-making technique." But such pronouncements are uninformative and would probably leave you skeptical and unsatisfied.

On the other hand, it's difficult to demonstrate fully how potent a tool this concept can be without moving into flow charts, decision trees, do loops, and other esoterica of the programmer's world. Let me try, however, to give you, through a few examples, a general idea of how this feature can be used.

A typical example is putting items in numerical order. Suppose you want to produce an inventory report for your business, printed with the stock numbers in sequence, smallest one first. You get two stock numbers at a time into the computer and must then determine which is smaller. So you subtract one from the other. The difference between two stock numbers doesn't have much significance, and you're not interested in the number you get as an answer. You can, however, use the sign indicator, the 1 or 0 at the left end, to set up the computer so that the smaller number will be identified and switched to the printer first. If you assign numerical values to the letters of the alphabet, you can use the same technique to put words in alphabetical order.

In case your reaction is that the preceding examples are neither impressive nor powerful, a competent programmer will be glad to demonstrate a more interesting use.

Having had such great success in wallpapering your living room with the aid of the computer, you decide to make use of it in your business. All your competitors are doing it, and you don't want to fall behind in the application of modern technology. You seek out the programmer who helped you with the wallpaper and state your request.

"I manage a business that has a large number of salesmen. I am having difficulties with the payroll calculation, and would like to enlist the aid of the computer."

"No problem," says the programmer. "Tell me, do you pay your salesmen by commission or salary?"

"Both. Some are paid one way, some the other."

"I see. That creates some minor complications, but it's no problem. I'll write a separate program for each kind, and we can run them through the computer separately."

"I'd rather, if you don't mind, sir, do them both at the same time. Computer time is expensive and using it only once should be more efficient. Besides, the computer can make decisions, can't it? Why not let it decide which program to use for each salesman?"

"Of course," says the programmer, a bit less confidently. "That will be no problem. I'll call you when I've worked it out."

You leave, and the programmer goes to his rampart, where he paces slowly back and forth. Listen, as he soliloquizes.

"What's the problem so far? I have two kinds of salary plans to work with, one for salesmen on commission, one for those on straight salary.

"What do I need next? I need two programs, one for each kind of payroll. Assume it's done. They're written and stored away safely in memory.

"Now, how do I know which program to use for each salesman? I'll obviously have to identify them in some way.

"How do I do that? Let's see. Every employee already has a number. Suppose I add another digit at the end of that number. I'll use a 7 for those on commission, and a 9 to mean salary.

"Next, after I read in the punched card for each employee, I'll subtract 8 from that last digit.

"And what will that do for me? Well, I'll be subtracting

the 8 from either 7 or 9, since those are the only two possible values for the last digit. Therefore, if the result of subtracting 8 is positive, the salesman's code must be 9; he's on salary, so I switch to that program. If the result of the subtraction is negative, the digit must have been a 7, so I switch to the commission calculation. Say, that's very good. I've found a way to have the computer decide which payroll program to use for each salesman."

In the language of computers, he's telling the truth. He has programmed the machine to make a decision. What's more, he can perform the same wonder in any number of other cases. He can make the computer decide when a credit limit is exceeded, how an airplane wing should be shaped to perform best at a given speed. He can even, if he has more than average ability, "teach" it to play chess. Once he figures out how to reduce the board, the pieces, and the competitive positions to a series of numbers, he can program the machine to decide which is the best move to make in that ancient and challenging game. As long as he can define two sets of instructions to be followed, depending on the outcome of a subtraction, he can have the computer make any decision you care to name.

What you have to reach your own conclusions about is this: even accepting the remarkable power and versatility of this function of the computer, how willing are you to call it decision making? Before you answer that question, let me once again remind you that the logic machine can be programmed to do anything that can be done logically. In other words, if logic permitted a different way to make decisions, then the computer could do it. But there is no other way. If you want to make decisions purely logically, that's how you have to make them, or it's as close as you can come.

So we seem to have come up against another limitation of the computer, and also of logic, just as we did in problem solving.

If you review the decisions you are forced to make from time to time you will find some cases where that mechanical routine fits your needs very well indeed. You can use it to decide whether or not to itemize the deductions on your income tax return, what kind of bank account will give you the best financial return, or whether the train is cheaper than the bus.

But the crop is a meager one. It doesn't include most of the significant decisions you must make in real life. Whom should you vote for? Should you move to that job in another city? Should you let your son drive the new car? None of these or the countless others like them can be reduced to a problem in subtraction with totally defined alternative courses of action. Life doesn't work like that. And some of us are glad it doesn't, while some of us wish it did.

6

The Power of Little Things

HOW do you measure the importance of a machine? What standard of judgment do you use to decide that this one is trivial, that one is important, and the other is of major significance?

You can't use the simple criterion of whether or not the machine causes social changes, because they all do that. In fact, to say that tools and machines have an impact on our way of life is a redundancy, since the reason we make such things in the first place is that we want to change the way we live. We are dissatisfied with our relationship with the environment, so we build something, whether it's a shelter, a weapon, or a wheel, that will alter the interaction.

Neither can you depend on the amount of public clamor a new technology creates. I hear a lot of talk about the way technology is upsetting our old ways, and I notice that it is generally restricted to such conspicuous examples as television, jet aircraft, the atom bomb, and the computer.

Such talk always makes me think of my mother, who had a different view in regard to mechanical things. To her, the greatest man who ever lived was the unknown genius who made the first washing machine—surely, she felt, the greatest invention of all time. And in terms of the benefits it brought her, she was quite correct. Her outlook may seem naive, but think for a moment of the impact of that mundane machine.

The washing machine and its mates in the laundries and kitchens of the world took the backbreaking toil out of the housewife's job, to the point where it is now surely one of the most automated occupations in the world. By doing so, didn't technology contribute an essential ingredient to the search by women for a new role in life? Weren't those inventions a major cause of the present turmoil in the relations between the sexes? Didn't those humble machines affect our society as much as the automobile did? Yet I never hear anyone point to household appliances as technology run wild or propose that we limit or abolish them. Public attention is not a reliable measure of a machine's significance.

So how do you measure the importance of a machine? Although I sometimes wonder whether it isn't a futile exercise, I raise the question because I'm now going to declare, without any supporting arguments, that the computer is not merely an important machine but is, by any method of ranking you care to use, one of the most significant tools that has ever been developed.

This estimate of its importance may appear to be inconsistent with the way I've been describing it—a dumb piece of hardware made up of little electronic elements, which can, if you give the right things the right names, simulate the most elementary logic operations. And a single basic logic operation like the one we did with those switches in chapter 2 doesn't seem to take you very far along the road to a technical revolution. That baby logic machine wasn't very impressive, and it certainly didn't have any obvious social significance. But little things can become highly important under the right set of conditions.

Consider, if you will, a single electron. Its vital statistics are thoroughly unimposing. It has a mass about 1/1800 of the hydrogen atom's and an electrical charge of about 1.6×10^{-19} coulombs. Those numbers are so small that they can't even be measured without elegant laboratory apparatus. They are small enough to make the electron appear to be a completely insignificant and useless entity. In fact, it is so unobtrusive that humanity coexisted with it for countless millenniums without ever knowing that it was there.

But when you learn how to make enough electrons, each carrying its minute charge, move through enough miles of wire, you suddenly have a form of energy that has changed our world and our society in every conceivable way. Electricity has become as indispensable, as much a part of our lives, as the ground under our feet, and it is based entirely on that infinitesimally tiny electron.

The transformation of the insignificant into the powerful is achieved, in the case of electricity, by the sheer number of those subatomic mysteries in any material. There are so many countless legions of them that the combination of their inconceivably small energies can light cities and move mountains.

In much the same way, trivial, unimpressive logic operations, when enough of them are used correctly, have the capacity to affect our lives to the same degree that electricity does. In this case, the catalyst that transforms insignificant elements into massive power is the speed at which the computer circuits operate.

To say that computers are incredibly fast is a gross understatement. They work in a time scale that is so far beyond the human experience as to be completely incomprehensible, except in a most shallow academic sense. As with astronomical distances, the numbers involved can be handled only as abstract ideas with little connection to our sense of reality. Still, recognizing the hazards of trying to comprehend the incomprehensible, let me try to put it into some perspective.

The basic unit for measuring time is the second. We're all familiar with it and have a rough idea of how long a period it is. Like all basic measurement units, the second is divided into smaller pieces identified by a set of prefixes: milli- for one thousandth, micro- for one millionth, and nano- for one billionth. A nanosecond, then, is one billionth of a second and it is the primary unit that computer designers use for measuring time.

If you ever get the chance to eavesdrop on a bunch of computer engineers, you will hear them talk glibly and casually about the nanosecond, as though they actually comprehended exactly what it is. But they don't really. It's just a unit of measure that they use in their work and never think about very much. Its real meaning is as mind-boggling to them as it is to you. How can anyone feel at home with the length of time it takes a car going sixty miles an hour to travel one millionth of an inch?

Inside the computer, the nanosecond finds its most common use as the unit for specifying the speed of the basic circuits. The important thing for the designer to know is how long it takes from the time that one circuit receives its input signals to the time that its output is, in turn, able to operate the next circuit. It is a significant measure because this time lag is the factor that limits the speed at which a sequence of those simple logical steps can take place inside the machine. It is a fairly good indicator of the ultimate speed of any computer.

Ordinary, relatively modest computers in production today use circuits that react in something like 20 nanoseconds. The circuits in the more elaborate, high-speed machines are roughly three times faster, working in about 6 nanoseconds. In the research laboratories there are devices that show promise of being one thousand times faster still. For the present we'll stay with the slower computers and say that a simple logic operation, like the one our AND circuit did, can be done with a time delay of 20 nanoseconds from input to output.

Twenty nanoseconds. Twenty billionths of a second. Hold that number in your mind for a moment and look at it from another angle. If you were to start today on the job of counting off a billion seconds, by the time you finished you would be 31 years older than you are now. So a nanosecond is the same fraction of 1 second as 1 second is of 31 years. To get a measure of what 20 nanoseconds is, count off 20 seconds, compare that interval of time to a 31-year slice of your life, and you have an idea of the fraction of a second in which those simple circuits work. If you feel more at home with big numbers than with little ones, another way of describing those circuits is to say that they can do fifty million logic functions in one second.

But of what earthly use to anyone is a circuit that can do fifty million logic operations in a second? The answer is mixed. As an isolated element such a circuit is of no use whatsoever. But enough of them put together create a tool so fast that it can be used with what may seem to be the grossest inefficiency and still provide a capability of unprecedented power. To put some substance into that statement, let's see what happens when some of those units are assembled into working blocks.

If a computer designer is handed a box full of those circuits, one of the things he will want to use them for would, as we know, be arithmetic. Since all arithmetic in a computer is done by some variation of addition, the basic design problem is to build an adder, something that will form the sum of two digits. The job of making an adder out of those little logic elements is actually an interesting but totally unglamorous problem, something you could acquire a detailed understanding of with just a few hours' work. What complicates it is all the auxiliary steps that have to be taken first—for example, getting the numbers changed into electrical signals that represent numbers in their binary form. But these and the other technical details that must be accounted for in practice are not relevant to the problem. Consider them all done.

When you string the logic elements together in the correct way to form the sum of two numbers, the result will be an assemblage in which the interconnected basic circuits are piled five layers deep. Since it takes 20 nanoseconds for a signal to get through each circuit, it will work its way through those five layers in 5 × 20 or 100 nanoseconds. The sum will start coming out of the back end of the adder 100 nanoseconds after the two numbers start to go in the front end. Another way of expressing it is that you have a collection of circuits able to add ten million pairs of digits in one second.

That's how fast the adder is, at least theoretically. But an adder is clearly of no use to anyone unless it has numbers to work with. Where will so many numbers come from, and where will the sum go? Answer, the computer's memory. And there you have the first bottleneck.

In most computers, the memory works in fixed cycles, operating in a regular, periodic time interval during which you can store or retrieve a certain number of those groups of 1s and 0s. Computers of the kind I'm talking about have memories that need about 1 microsecond to go through a cycle. They can handle numbers going in or coming out at the rate of 1 million per second, which means that 1,000 nanoseconds are being used up for every cycle and by your new standards of speed that should begin to sound like a long time. In fact, since one such cycle is needed to get the numbers from the memory to the adder and another cycle to put the result back, we have raised the actual adding time from the theoretical 100 nanoseconds to a more realistic 2,000, a loss of speed of 20 to 1. Already you can visualize the adder sitting there most of the time humming to itself and tapping its fingers impatiently.

The situation gets even worse. In actual practice you have to take care of such vital steps as getting the ADD instruction from the memory, figuring out what it is, and setting it up. Throw in a few more technical odds and ends that must be taken care of, and you have extended the time for addition to about four memory cycles, or 4,000 nanoseconds. In going from the basic adder to the final result you have lost about 97 percent of the potential capacity of the adder. It is working the equivalent of one day out of each month. But despite such shocking indolence, the machine can add a quarter of a million pairs of digits in a second.

The computer engineer beams with pride at this point, but his pride is short-lived. He still hasn't solved the problem of feeding the fantastic appetite of the machine. While he now has the memory and all the other parts of the computer marching in step, he faces still another barrier. How does he get all those numbers in and out of the memory?

Part of the answer is that many of the numbers with which the machine is working never enter or leave the computer. Much computer arithmetic involves using the result of one calculation, such as the partial total of a column of numbers, in another calculation. But even so, if the potential speed of the machine is to be even partially realized, great quantities of data must somehow be shuttled in and out as quickly as possible.

The most efficient way to do that is by using a magnetic recording medium in the form of tape or disks. These units provide an extension of the computer's memory, and their speed is, at first glance, impressive. They can absorb or spew out information, such as numbers, at the rate of about 100,000 per second.

Not bad for mechanical gadgets, but ten times slower

than the electronic memory, and you can see how it reduces the efficiency with which you're using the adder. To make matters worse, these mechanisms must be started and stopped as determined by the computer program, and here is where their innate sluggishness is most frustrating.

For example, when the computer runs out of numbers to work with and has to go out to get more, it takes three thousandths or four thousandths of a second for the magnetic tape to start moving. In some circles that might seem like a fairly prompt response, but it means that for 3,000 or 4,000 memory cycles the computer is doing nothing but wait. And a punched-card reader or a printer takes far longer than that to move.

So you have an imbalance. On the one hand, you have the incredible internal speed of the computer, and on the other the merely fantastic performance of the "peripheral equipment," the electromechanical devices through which the computer is fed and voided. The problem has been an aggravation from the beginning. It has meant that every computer must have a built-in idling mode, during which it waits for something to come in from the outside. And it didn't take much experience with even the earliest systems to discover that the computer was spending a horrifying percentage of its time in that unproductive state. It could be compared to a racing car with a fuel tank so small that it has to be refilled every few minutes.

To counter this disturbing state of affairs, engineers turned their attention to the mechanical units, especially to the printers and the magnetic tape and disk units. Their achievements were, in themselves, minor miracles of precision and speed, pushing the capabilities of mechanical pieces to their very limits. But every time the mechanisms were improved, the electronics made an equivalent advance, so the disparity remained. When it finally became clear that it always would remain, the engineers and programmers set out to find other ways to put all that wasted computer time to constructive use. The basic approach they've taken has been to load the computer with more than one job, so that when one program is forced to wait for something mechanical to happen, the computer is switched to another job instead of just goofing off for all those milliseconds. While it is waiting the fraction of a second it takes the printer to move the paper to the next line of the inventory report, it might as well be computing a couple of circuit equations for the engineering department. And that's what it does.

The "throughput"—computer jargon for the amount of useful work the machine can do—is increased by this maneuver, but, as for everything else in life, you pay a price. Instructions must now be added to keep track of the different jobs and to switch the computer from one program to another, and these steps use up some of the time you're saving.

But in spite of all the inefficiencies you have a machine whose ability to do arithmetic is limited only by the speed with which you can shovel the numbers in and out. And while numerical operations have been used as an example, they are only one example. There are many other things that the computer is designed to do in support of the programmer's goals, and in every case the same thing happens. You start with a set of supremely fast logic elements, string them together to perform some required function, arrange to get the necessary data in and out of the memory and then in and out of the machine. At each step you lose some of the speed you started out with, but in the end you still have a time scale so far beyond your own as to give you one of the most awesome machines ever created, one whose uses and abuses seem to be unlimited.

It can be programmed to design windshield wipers and to run a hot-dog factory, to forecast election results and to make up payolls. It can be used to design quieter jet engines and to set type for newspapers. It can help teach retarded children to read and bill you for the restaurant meals you enjoyed last month without any money.

In addition, it dislocates legions of workers while creating hundreds of thousands of new and different jobs. Its careless use causes endless grief with ridiculous bills, mistaken identities, and incomprehensible cards which you mustn't fold, staple, or mutilate. It will help you and it will bedevil you. But most of all it will come to loom in people's minds as a vague but oppressive menace, one whose mere existence seems to stir a little tremor of fear that few machines before it have roused.

Those problems are of great concern to everyone. Before we start to nibble at them, let me just remind you that we didn't set out on this quest to get into such major issues, but merely to see what a simple little logic operation with two switches and a light bulb can lead to. It turns out to be not so insignificant after all.

But the computer remains a machine, built by people and understandable by people. As a matter of fact, you now know enough about its workings to understand how it relates to people and how it may fit into our society. Since most of the interest in the computer stems from its image as a latent artificial intelligence and much of the apprehension it creates comes from its potential as a competitor for your job, those are the major areas we will explore. In both cases the key to the problem is a comparison between what the computer can do and what people can do, and for this we need first to find out what the experts have learned about that fascinating entity, the human brain.

7

Many Schools of Thought

EVERYTHING about science makes us look to the future, but there is one branch of it that, for me, is pure nostalgia. Whenever I venture into the part of the academic world where people are trying to explain to one another how the brain works, I am transported back to the old-fashioned city street markets that I knew as a child. There is the same bewildering variety of offerings. The air is filled with the sounds of the same arguments, expressed more elegantly but with just as much passion.

What's being sold in this intellectual marketplace is answers to questions that have always fascinated people. How does the mass inside the skull do its thing? How does it run the body, sense the world, communicate with other minds, wonder at its own functioning?

The booths and counters offering solutions crowd each other side by side. As you stroll among them, the materialist and the spiritualist, the scientist and the mystic, the atheist and the believer shout their wares for you to come and see. Your support is solicited by biochemists, philosophers, engineers, psychologists, theologians, physicists, and doctors, to name only a few.

The market opened for business hundreds of years ago,

and there has never been a shortage of people anxious to set up shop. The turnover is high, since most of the theories go out of business in a few years for lack of customers. But as soon as one bright idea disappears, the empty space is occupied by another. The street is as full of controversy today as it ever was, and as it probably will be for hundreds of years to come.

The uncounted theories about how we think which have been offered over the centuries can be roughly categorized as falling into two opposing camps. On the one side are those who believe in a mechanical solution to the problem. Just as physics has shown that the smallest falling stone and the largest distant star both move according to the same orderly, mathematically organized laws, so must the brain also be explainable in terms of masses, energies, and forces. Nothing beyond the measurable and the testable can exist. There is no basic difference between the physical and the mental, except that the equations for the one have already been found; those for the other eventually will be.

The second school believes that there is a basic difference between body and mind. The problems of consciousness and awareness cannot be totally answered by the equations of motion or of equivalent circuits. Mathematical physics may work for inert masses, but living things cannot be analyzed or understood by way of the same approach.

There are a large number of variations and combinations of those beliefs; that is why there are so many theories to choose from. But the division is accurate enough for our purposes. And don't conclude that it is between theologians on one side and scientists on the other. You will find people of all persuasions on both sides of the street.

The first computer had hardly been warmed up before it was swept into the center of the controversy. Here, the claim went, was a machine that could do arithmetic, sort and process data, evaluate alternatives, solve problems. What could be more natural than to see it as the mechanical counterpart of the brain? And so a subdivision of the science of computers was born and given the name of research into artificial intelligence, abbreviated to AI. Its purpose, briefly put, is to make the computer show behavior which, beyond any argument, can be called intelligent. It has been the subject of concentrated attention by highly talented people for many years, and, following the natural evolution of all specialties, it has developed its own experts, its own journals, and its own jargon.

Only modest attention was ever paid to the work by the commercial side of the computer industry, so my own job never involved me in the research. But I was always interested, and I assigned myself the task of keeping fairly close track of what was happening. As one part of that effort, I attended a series of seminars at a major university, in which active researchers reported on the progress of their intensive work in the subject. I went to those seminars intermittently over a period of about ten years, starting in the late 1950s, and was fascinated by the way they changed during that time.

In the early years, the researchers saw nothing but smooth sailing ahead. A typical lecture started with a slide showing the outline of a human head, much like those so popular with the makers of TV commercials. Inside the head, occupying the area usually reserved for clogged sinuses, was a sketch of a telephone switchboard, complete with a little operator busily making connections.

The problem, we were told, was pretty well under control. Signals, in electrical form, travel along the nervous system from various parts of the body. In the brain, the signals are processed, switched through to other paths of the system, and sent whistling happily along their way to do whatever chore is required of them. In addition (next slide, please), we have a box up here that acts as the overall controller and one here to store the information and the control program. How could anyone deny that the brain was just like a computer?

The researchers had even figured out how the logic elements worked. They had found the biological equivalents of the AND, OR, and NOT circuits of a computer. Granted, there were some differences in the detailed functioning, what with thresholds and so on, but the same things could be done with electronics. All that remained, admittedly difficult but not theoretically impossible, was to trace out some of the more interesting switching functions of the mind, duplicate them with electronic circuits, and there you were, artificial intelligence (AI).

Ten years later, at the last of the seminars I attended, the picture was totally different. The outlined head was gone, apparently shipped back in disgrace to the patent-medicine peddlers. Gone was the feeling that the problem had been solved, gone was the easy comparison of axons and neurons to diodes and transistors. Instead of offering the right answers, the speakers were groping for the right questions. The research had grown ten years older and become fifty years more humble. The confident assault on the fortress inside the human head had been called off on account of no progress. It was time to regroup for the next attack.

The research which has been done, and which is continuing, has been of great value. Out of it came substantial improvements in computer equipment and programs, improvements which inevitably found their way into commercial systems. But in the pursuit of making the computer act like the human mind, there have probably been more retreats than advances.

The progression from confidence to humility is typical of the history of the effort to understand how the brain works. Time after time, enthusiastic scientists have charged in, brandishing their bright ideas like cavalry swords. Surely this time the problem would crumble under the onslaught of science and reason. Later, when the dust had settled, they would emerge, tired but not beaten. They would say something like: "It turned out to be more complicated than I had anticipated. But I remain confident that the direction I have pointed out is the correct one. If someone else will pick up the challenge and carry on the effort, I'm sure my ideas will prevail." In the meantime, the problem has continued to resist the most ingenious and stubborn attempts to unlock the mystery.

That's not really a correct statement. The frustrating part of the problem is that it doesn't resist, it doesn't put up a struggle. Instead, it behaves like a mattress you are trying to push up a stairway. Wherever you apply effort, it gives, it yields. But no matter how hard you push and shove, no matter how it bends under your exertion, the damn thing doesn't move. In the same way, the brain yields gracefully to any theory you care to propose about how it works. If you wish to view it as an electrical switching system, there is plenty of evidence to reassure you that, yes indeed, it is a switching system. If you prefer to see it as a complex chemical porridge in which ions are traded back and forth and huge molecules dance and change shape, there are all sorts of tests you can make to verify your ideas. If your tastes run to electromagnetic theories, you can find lots of interactions to prove that you're on the right trail, and maybe only a little more work is needed to prove it.

But while there is evidence to show that all the theories are right, there is also evidence to show that not one of them is adequate. So far, every idea on how that gray mass functions has proved totally incapable of explaining more than a tiny part of the puzzle. Every one of them runs out of steam and eventually falls far short of solving the problem of how the parts of the brain work.

The same frustration exists at the higher level, when you try to fathom, not the mechanics of how the pieces function, but how the system works as a whole, how we use it to form thoughts. For that matter, we don't even know what a thought is. Is it a physical thing like a finger or a nerve, which, if you could find it, you could pick up and look at and measure and take pictures of? Or is a thought just a temporary change in a medium, like the picture on a television tube, a momentary flaring of phosphorescence as the electron beam races across the screen? Don't be too eager to answer that multiple-choice question. The correct response may be A or B or both or neither. Nobody knows.

The elusiveness of such basic problems drives scientists to distraction. They can't bring themselves to believe that the basic laws of chemistry and physics and electricity fail to apply, and apparently they're right. There are no anomalies. No one has ever found unknown chemical elements in the brain. Electrons follow the same rules there that they do in transistors. There are no violations of the laws of conservation of energy or of thermodynamics. But so far, the laws of physics have totally failed to explain how it all comes together to work. All the pieces are the right shape, but they still won't fit together.

So elusive is the target that it often isn't even possible to disprove other people's theories about the brain. Take, for example, the ancient idea that the inert physical components by themselves are useless, that only the addition of a nonphysical ingredient explains the workings of the human mind. The idea is that the parts of the brain, like the plates of a storage battery, are nothing until they are "charged." To perform that function, you postulate something like a soul, a life force, or a spirit. Such ideas don't sit well with a lot of scientists, but how in the world can they contradict them?

Surgeons have been quoted as saying such things as "I've worked on a great many living brains, but I've never seen anything in them that looks like a soul." Sounds convincing, but if they mean to imply that nothing can exist in the brain unless they can see it, their reasoning is bad. In the course of their probing and cutting, they have never seen a fresh new idea, a prejudice, or a witty saying, but it would be foolish to conclude that none of these exist. Lack of physical presence doesn't prove or disprove anything about what's going on inside the cranium. As far as I can tell, the idea of a soul fits the known facts about the mind just as well as any other theory I've come across.

We have a basic body of chemical and electrical facts about what goes on inside the head. We have a rough knowledge of which parts of the brain perform what functions. We have a large bank of information about the many faces of behavior. But the mystery of how it all works remains as deep today as it was when the first philosopher began to wonder about it. Whether it will ever be resolved remains to be seen, but keep an open mind on the question. In the meantime, be aware of the fact that when it comes to explaining intelligence all you can get is opinions and theories.

Announcing that all theories of intelligence are speculation may be an odd way to introduce my own ideas on the subject, but that's exactly what I'm doing. One more peddler is setting up his stand and hawking his wares.

Before you turn up your nose and hurry by without even pausing to look at the merchandise, let me grab you by the sleeve and explain why it makes sense to offer one more theory in an already glutted market. Basically it is because the arguments in support of the position that a computer can think are too strong to be ignored.

Despite all the setbacks and dead ends in the attempt to create an intelligent machine, there is no doubt that much of what the computer does was once the sole domain of the human mind. It does encroach into areas that have always been regarded as thinking, and more is involved than a tricky use of words. Regardless of how it's done—by giving the right name to a voltage or whatever—you can indeed use the computer to do your arithmetic, to control complex production processes, to do any number of jobs which have always been viewed as requiring some degree of intelligence. You can't just shrug off these facts as irrelevant or dismiss them as an exercise in sophistry.

It doesn't do much good, either, to try to pin down the kind of specific task you will ask for as a demonstration of intelligence. Without a good theory underpinning the selection of jobs, you can easily make the wrong choice. Time after time, skeptics have said things like "The computer will never play a decent game of chess." Time after time the computer has eventually been programmed to do exactly what was asked for. The skeptics who took that approach have been in constant retreat.

What I would like to do instead is to see whether a limit to the machine's potential can be found. Can a line be drawn, up to which we can say the machine is capable of being used, but beyond which it will never be able to go? That's exactly the task I propose to undertake with the simple theory I bring to the market.

I offer my theory with one proviso, though. Don't take it as a serious attempt to explain the functioning of the mind. All I want to do is sharpen the picture of what the computer is and what it is not. I don't know how the brain works, but I do know how the computer works, and I can't visualize any way they could be the same. My goal is not to solve any of the mysteries of the mind but to try to provide a little insight into how the computer relates to them.

The line of reasoning is very simple. The roots of the theory lie in renaming the computer the logic machine, because it can be used to perform any function made up of purely logical steps and can do nothing else. The next ingredient is the conclusions we reached when we explored the myths that computers solve problems and make decisions. There are implications to those conclusions which should now be explored.

Consider the case of decision making. You probably accepted quite happily the news that the computer can only make a decision by blindly subtracting one number from another. But I suspect that your reaction will be somewhat different when you are told that the same restriction applies to you when you make your own decisions.

The case, you will probably protest, is overdrawn. You don't make decisions by comparing two numbers, but you do make decisions logically. You must, because there simply are no other respectable ways of deciding things. Just look at the dismal options you have if you don't use logic. You can toss a coin, follow a hunch, disembowel a sheep, obey an impulse, or cast your horoscope. None of them is your style; you disapprove of the whole list. Surely, between the mechanical subtraction of the computer on the one hand and the unsoundness of the alternatives on the other, there must be a middle ground?

But there isn't. Pure logic works the same way the computer does, and vice versa. You can't change that fact, however much you might like to.

Once you find that logic can cope only with solutions and not with problems and can make decisions only in the narrowly restricted sense of subtraction, you are faced with an obvious question: how do people make decisions? The only answer I can think of is that we humans must have additional faculties. We can do things that logic can't, so we must have some other thinking tools at our disposal.

While the argument seems straightforward and convincing to me, I know that many will find it hard to accept.

Despite its obvious shortcomings, logic has come to have an unassailable reputation as the sole carrier of intelligence in the human mind. Regardless of how it may have happened, logic and intelligence have become so synonymous that when the logic machine came along it seemed rather obvious to follow a line of thinking like this:

1. The computer is a logic machine.
2. Logic equals intelligence.
3. Therefore the computer is an intelligence machine.

If you were to ask me to work out that syllogism on the little machine we built, I would set switch 1 to the up position: that statement is true. But switch 2 would stay down and the light would stay off. Statement 2 is false and so is the conclusion. There has to be more to intelligence than just logic.

That, in essence, is the basis for my simplistic theory of the human mind: to state that we must have other thinking faculties in addition to logic and to make a rather arbitrary decision on what they are.

In order to identify what those other faculties may be, go back and reconsider some of those unacceptable decision-making alternatives in a new light. Throw out tossing a coin, examining the entrails of a sheep, and astrology. Even if you use them all the time for tough decisions, they aren't among the alternatives I care to pursue. But look at the other two, hunches and impulse, to see what value they may have as thinking mechanisms.

For a number of reasons I'm going to call them intuition and emotion, though I realize that using those names will make very little difference in your willingness to accept them. Intuition you know to be unreliable, just a small step beyond tossing a coin. And emotion is even worse. You have learned that making emotional decisions is a habit to be shunned at all times. To admit to it is to admit to a less rational and intelligent level of thinking than you would care to confess to in public.

With such reputations, my calling these faculties vital ingredients in human thinking will be insufficient to convince you. The next step must be to find out what they do for us that logic can't. We all recognize them as facets of human personality, but we will have to establish that they are essential to the thinking process, rather than merely being quaint human weaknesses which will some day be bred out of the species as no longer necessary to intelligent life.

I realize that defending human foibles like emotion and intuition does not fall within the area of expertise usually assigned by society to the engineer. It really belongs to the psychologist, and nothing makes people close their minds more quickly than does the prospect of a specialist's starting to sound off in a specialty other than his own. Our society expects an expert to be highly territorial, to refrain from straying into the other fellow's preserve and to fight off any incursion into his own.

Psychology is a particularly sensitive area, because it is the specialty most subject to intrusion by the layman. It is, after all, the study of the behavior of people, and we all have the opportunity, indeed the need, to develop some knowledge about that subject. Not many of us, in our daily lives, find it necessary to know anything about electron energy levels, deoxyribonucleic acid, or Hittite artifacts, but we all have a great deal of contact with people and are, in fact, encouraged to learn more and more about them.

Still, we aren't supposed to work outside our classification, and for a long time I was reluctant to venture onto the uncertain ground of explaining people to one another. But that inhibition was removed a number of years ago, in the intellectually stimulating environment of the company cafeteria. One day, as I chewed unenthusiastically on the egg-flavored cardboard that was the Sandwich du Jour, I listened to two engineers deep in a discussion about one of the less popular supervisors.

"You know," George remarked, "he'd be a good man if he could only redirect his aggressions into more positive outlets. He's obviously compensating for a deep-seated feeling of inadequacy, probably realizes, subconsciouswise, that he's unqualified for the job he's in."

"Oh, come off it!" said Sam. "What the hell's going on these days? Everybody's an amateur psychologist."

George thought for a moment, then nodded. "Yeah. And that includes the professionals."

Since that time I have been an occasional but enthusiastic player in what is probably our most popular national sport.

Yet, while parlor psychology is an acceptable way to pass an idle hour over a friendly drink, to offer your musings for public consideration is something else again. Nor are the academic qualifications I bring to the problem very impressive. My record includes no degrees in psychology, earned or honorary, no graduate seminars, no undergraduate electives. I've never even owned any white mice. And as if stepping on psychologists' toes weren't enough, I'll also be encroaching on the territory of the philosopher. Here, though, my credentials are somewhat better: I did once take a course in the subject. These disclaimers are offered, not to apologize for my brashness in tackling those topics, but rather to warn you that in dealing with emotion and intuition we will be skimming over complex problems to which brilliant and dedicated people have devoted lifetimes of intensive study.

But skimming over deep waters has its rewards too. Most of the life in the ocean exists only because of the organisms to be found in the top few inches of water. There's a lot of value in looking only at that small portion, so long as you don't start to believe that you have become an expert in what goes on in the depths.

Skimming will be quite adequate. It is all we need in order to proceed with this theory, because once we have an understanding of what each of the three faculties—logic, emotion, and intuition—contributes to our intelligence, we can piece together a picture of human thinking that puts the computer in its proper place with respect to people.

8

Logic Revisited

I'VE had quite a bit to say up to now about how inadequate logic is to account for all of our intelligence. But it's important not to go to the other extreme and decide to pitch logic overboard entirely. Logic is much more than a diabolical instrument that engineers and similar fussbudgets use to infuriate normal people.

It can't be dismissed, either, as merely a passing fad, something overly admired during this brief moment of history by a society enamored of science and technology. Logic as a way of thinking has been endlessly tested over the years and has shown astonishing durability. In its long trek from Aristotle to the data bank it passed through many generations and through a bewildering range of civilizations. In every time, in every place, in every language, it has been scrutinized and probed. In every case its validity and value were verified. Few other ideas have been transferred through so many different cultures and emerged so nearly intact.

Can anything, even a religion, pass from one culture to another for so long without some kind of significant change? In the case of logic, the answer is "almost." It's true that during the course of the centuries-long study some minor modifications were made. The nomenclature was changed somewhat, the rules were made more formal, but the basic structure stayed exactly the same.

The old ideas faced their greatest challenge in a movement that started in the middle 1800s and probably isn't finished yet. The critique did not start with the logicians, who were still happily picking through the works of the old masters to see what nuggets others might have missed, but with the mathematicians, who by that time had an uneasy feeling that the increasingly elegant structure they had built rested on shaky foundations. They decided that they needed much better and more rigorous proofs to bolster the work they had inherited from Newton and Leibniz and the other fathers of their art.

George Boole's book, which showed that logic could be treated in the same way as algebra, came along at about that time and promptly threw logic into the pot for its share of criticism. The movement then turned into a concentrated and totally uninhibited re-examination of the entire basis of all mathematical and logical thinking. Every old idea in those studies became a candidate for careful scrutiny and possible rejection. All the great names of mathematics were subjected to the massive critique, and so was Aristotle, whose name could no longer evoke instant agreement.

The results of all the upheaval changed the face of mathematics. Out of it came the theory of sets, which, for some reason, is now used to introduce schoolchildren to simple mathematics, as well as totally different kinds of algebra and strange new geometries in which parallel lines can meet, geometries which Einstein later used to formulate his theory of relativity.

In much the same way the theory behind Aristotle's logic system was so radically modified that the old master would have had to go back to school to learn it and might well have flunked in the effort. An entirely different approach was taken, with statements and words replaced by strange new symbols. Simple examples like "All men are human" were thrown away in favor of abstractions of the highest order. To the logicians nothing stayed the same. Their ancient discipline had been altered almost beyond recognition.

While all this commotion was important to mathematicians and logicians, most people still don't know or care that it happened, and for a very good reason. Despite its world-shaking significance to the people involved in the work, none of it had any direct effect on the average individual.

The experts, for example, tackled the surprisingly difficult task of trying to define what a number is and came up with a rather tortuous one couched in terms of the theory of sets. That achievement may have put a better theoretical foundation under all mathematics, but when you sit down to balance your bank statement, the definition of a number is as irrelevant as it ever was. You still use the same addition and subtraction that you struggled so hard to master, and you still get the correct answer if you use them properly. Mathematics has changed dramatically, but arithmetic has not changed at all.

And so it is with logic. Its theoretical foundations have been altered beyond recognition, but for ordinary people trying to think their way through the real events of the real world, Aristotle's logic has survived virtually intact.

For our purposes, the major result of the long and intensive soul-searching by the experts was the fusion of mathematics and logic into a single package. What had historically always been treated as two separate, unrelated studies was now seen as a single unified one.

This extension of Boole's idea is the foundation on which the computer's importance is based. Before then, machines had been built to do, at best, simple calculation which was recognized as important, but still basically an accessory to human thinking. Devices like the abacus and slide rule obviously were not parallels of human thought.

But when the newly unified calculation and logic were embodied in a machine, an entirely different situation existed. The computer is designed, as you saw with our homemade AND gate, primarily to perform logical operations. Calculating is only a small part of what it can do, almost a sideline, as it is with people. By this implementation of logic, there came into being for the first time a machine that paralleled a highly respected and well-proven way of thinking, a machine that broke what had always before been a human monopoly.

The advent of some kind of logic machine was probably inevitable. Logic is inherently compatible with a completely mechanical analogue primarily because logic can be described by, in fact is governed by, a fixed set of rules. And logic is indeed a world of absolute and unyielding rules. It is a dictatorial umpire with whose decisions there is no argument. If you want to play the game of logic you follow the rules and you accept the results without question. There are no appeals, no exceptions, no favoritism.

Such inflexibility makes logic seem cold and lifeless to most people, and they are quite right—it really is cold and lifeless, possessing none of the qualities we think of as likable and human. But likable or not, its chill precision matches the way the physical universe functions. That is one of the major values of logic, one whose importance is difficult to overstate.

It's a long time since I heard anyone disagree with the idea that the physical universe runs in a way that can be unfailingly described by a set of mathematical equations. We are now so accustomed to the idea that it is easy to forget how much impact it had when it was born in the seventeenth century, how abruptly it departed from all mankind's previous pictures of how the world works.

There may still be some people who doubt the validity of this "mechanistic philosophy," and I don't intend to argue the issue but only to point out that the theory certainly works in practice. We saw its most spectacular vindication only recently, when a set of equations formulated three hundred years earlier by someone who never left England was proven totally correct on the trips to the moon and to Mars. I know of very few intellectual works of such cosmic reach and universality. The equations of physics may not be warm and friendly, they may have to be modified slightly every once in a while, but they certainly work.

You don't have to understand or even to know about those equations to be governed by them. They apply to a pirouetting ballerina, to the structure of a palm tree, to the rope bridges built by aborigines, to the flight of an insect, to the sound of a guitar string. The equations are valid whether we know them or not, whether we approve of them or not. They are there, they work, they must be obeyed.

Gravity, for example, works according to the appropriate equations all the time. The equations function to give a child a fun ride down a sliding board, and they work exactly the same way to kill the child if he leans too far out of a window. The mathematics and logic are always consistent and correct, regardless of whether or not the consequences are to our liking. That's how the world is, and logic is an absolutely necessary part of our intelligence if we are to understand and cope with it.

Scientists and engineers learn the lesson the hard way. There is a rule in physics about inertia, which says that the more massive a thing is, the more force it takes to make it move or make it stop, and there are mathematical equations defining this relationship with precision. When a young engineer overlooks them in the design of a gadget, the gadget won't work. He can object, he can cry, he can take to the streets with picket signs, but the fact of inertia will not go away and he has to recalculate his design to take it into account. The mathematics of the universe wins the battle every time.

After a few unsuccessful fights against facts like these and the logic that fits them so closely, the engineer stops struggling and will refuse even to listen to arguments on the subject. People then call him cold and precise and dry. He says he's simply recognizing reality. Both statements are true.

For all its mechanical, unfeeling nature, logic is of vital importance. It certainly fits the world of reality when it deals with such things as gravity—be careful around those open windows. It works infallibly in the world of science, and that's what we usually associate it with, but its value goes beyond mathematics and the workings of the physical universe.

There is good reasoning and there is bad reasoning in our everyday lives too. There is good reasoning and bad reasoning in our dealings with one another and with ourselves. The rules of logic sort them out for us, and we should know the rules and use them. Ignoring them or misusing them can lead us astray in all sorts of ways.

For example, if we generalize the syllogism we've been using up to now, it would look like this:

1. All A's are B's.
2. C is an A.
3. Therefore C is a B.

That is a valid logical statement according to the rules. You can try it against any of the previous examples and see how well it fits. But now change it slightly to look like this:

1. All A's are B's.
2. C is a B.
3. Therefore C is an A.

The rules say that this is not valid logic. You cannot claim that if statements 1 and 2 are true, it follows that statement 3 is true. If all this sounds obscure and complicated, just put in some specifics to clarify it.

All Lithuanians are human.
Socrates is human.
Therefore Socrates is a Lithuanian.

Obviously ridiculous. Obviously an invalid piece of logic. But do you remember this version of it?

All Communists read Karl Marx.
Joe reads Karl Marx.
Therefore Joe is a Communist.

From the point of view of the logic rules, it's exactly the same as the previous one and is no more valid. But it was a line of reasoning used by a lot of people to whom good logic was not the most important thing in the world.

To say that bad logic has caused a great deal of misery in the course of history would be to overstate the case. But twisted reasoning has been a common tool for the demagogue and the bigot, for anyone who has been more concerned with the sale of his ideas than with their validity. As such, bad logic has been, if not the cause, at least an active partner in a lot of nasty events.

Unfortunately, many people who notice that link fall prey to some illogic of their own. They decide that fixing up people's ability to think clearly would end the problem. If bad logic is associated with evil results, they reason, then good logic must lead to understanding and good will, as in "Come, let us reason together."

I'm afraid not. Good logic will not end any of the common hostilities or animosities among mankind. Logic is not common sense, it is not sweet reason, it is not willingness to see the other side of an argument, it is not a sense of fair play. Logic has nothing to do with the way we relate to other people or to their ideas. It has no connection with our being good or bad people, open-minded or bigoted, willing or unwilling to examine new ideas. Those are attributes that come from the assumptions with which you approach the world and the people in it. Being logical, by itself, says nothing about you as a person except that you know the rules and follow them.

The basic limitation of logic is that it only enables you to derive relationships between the assumptions you start with, the things you believe to be true or false. Everybody who ever brushed against logic in school knows that, but there's a strong tendency to forget it. In the days when Euclid's geometry was taught as the ultimate in logical thinking, those assumptions were called axioms—statements so obviously true as to need no proof. Nowadays, as a result of the work after Boole, they are called hypotheses, premises, or definitions, more modest words that say we'll consider certain statements to be true for the time being and maybe change our minds later.

Whatever you may call them, assumptions about what is true or not true provide the only "facts" with which logic can work, but they must come from somewhere else. All logic can do is to find the results that come from applying the logic rules to the assumptions you have made.

You saw that—in the flesh, so to speak—when you worked the switches of the little machine to find out if the U.S.A. is decadent. The mechanized logic merely "processed" the inputs you fed it, contributing nothing except its built-in rules. Nor do we need so modern an example to illustrate the relationship between logic and assumptions; it can be seen all the way back to the origins of the discipline.

Aristotle did not merely codify logic, he used it to build up theories about almost anything you care to name. They were developed with flawless and impressive logic, and they covered the whole range of human curiosity. For centuries those theories formed an unquestioned foundation on which whole structures of knowledge were based. Unfortunately many of them were wrong. It took a long time to discover that heavy things do not fall faster than light ones, or that the sun does not revolve around the earth, as Aristotle had concluded.

He went wrong primarily because he lived before the idea of the carefully controlled experiment was conceived. All he could do was observe the world and work out the logical implications of what he saw. The trouble is that simple observation, no matter how keen, can be misleading. After all, in air a stone does fall faster than a feather or a twig, and unless you do some very careful experimenting it may seem safe to assume that you have found a general rule. Since Aristotle had no way of experimentally checking the assumptions he made from his observations, many of his conclusions were logical and still dead wrong.

You would think that with so much history to show the weakness of logic used by itself, without contact with the real world, the hazard would be pretty well established in our minds. But now it crops up again in the form of a computer, and people still don't seem to recognize it.

Where the capability of logic is a source of confusion, the question of its merits is a source of strongly divided opinion. To some people the rigid, impersonal character of logic is the very thing that makes it attractive. Those who aspire to an orderly intellectual life are perpetually bothered by the chaotic and unruly world of human thinking. Logic's structured, timeless system is, to them, a haven of civilized behavior in an otherwise lawless wilderness. It is a place where disputes can be settled by reference to agreed-upon rules instead of by vitriolic argument, where physical combat yields to the structured beauty of mathematics.

While such discipline attracts some people, it actively repels others. In some cases they say it's because they object to being restricted by a set of abstract rules, even though they're fighting a futile battle: logic won't go away or cease being valid just because you may wish it would. But I often suspect that there is another reason. Logic is relentlessly honest, never bending to your wishes, never giving you an answer because it wants to please you. If you work through a sequence of logical thought and don't like what it tells you, you can't blame the logic or try to change it. If you want a result more pleasing to your taste or vanity, you must go back and look at the assumptions you made. Logic often forces you to recognize that you are working with bad premises, an exercise in introspection which is not always a pleasant experience. If there is one part of our intelligence that embodies the virtue and the difficulty of intellectual honesty, this is it.

9

An Emotional Appeal

EMOTION: n. Agitation of the feelings or sensibilities.

That doesn't sound so bad, does it? It isn't a word to strike terror into the hearts of the innocent, or to get you a punch in the mouth if you say it to a friend. The dictionaries that I looked it up in all defined it pretty much the same. They all place it on a scale of synonyms that goes something like: feeling, emotion, sentiment, and passion. If you prefer to use one of the other words, then make your own personal choice. Choose any one, that is, except passion; that's not what I'm talking about.

Ever since people first started expressing their thoughts about how someone else thinks, emotion has been recognized as being distinct and different from logic. Fine. Who can argue with that? But the recognition has generally led to categorizing people as thinking one way or the other. You are fuzzy-headed or hard-headed, feminine or masculine, a dreamer or a doer, a poet or a peasant.

Since the world is usually run by hard-headed male doers who claim to admire the solid peasant virtues, they have always been the ones who set the standards of what is good thinking. In the best human tradition, those standards reflected the way they would like to picture themselves. So, in most societies, there has always been the implication that feelings come lower in the intelligence hierarchy than logic does. And that's the windmill I've picked up my lance to attack.

I don't plan to write a dissertation on the causes, symptoms, and treatment of human emotion. I don't intend to lecture on love and hate, friendliness and hostility, aggression and timidity. I won't even touch on that most popular of emotional subjects, your sex life. There will be no graphic elucidation of how to master the ten most exotic and gratifying amatory techniques (system configurations, some engineers call them). All I want to do is to establish the intellectual value of emotion and identify some of the things it does that logic can't.

Look first at some of the obvious differences between the two. Start with the observation that, where logic is constant and universal, emotion is infinitely varied. The identical laws and syllogisms of logic apply to all of us all the time. One man's logic is the same as every other man's. But emotions are changeable and unpredictable. They vary widely from one person to another and, in the same person, from one time to another.

Where logic comes to us complete and unalterable, like a frozen dinner from the supermarket, emotion is a dish of our own making, a recipe we are constantly changing. Logic is a finished package whose contents we see only in their final form. It is prepared, labeled, and ready to use. You can take it or leave it, but you can't influence what went into it. On the other hand, we all cook up our emotional stew for ourselves. We all start out with the same basic ingredients, the drives for survival and reproduction, but all of us teach one another and learn from one another how to modify and build upon those ingredients. We influence one another's emotions with every contact we have, in a process that never ends. Unlike logic, our emotions are never a completed package.

Where logic had Aristotle to set down the basic rules, to state the laws that separate good logic from bad, emotion had—who? Take your pick from a large number of wise men, scholars, saints, and their opposites. While everybody who teaches logic has texts and references that basically agree, whose writings are correct and accepted in the world of emotions? You probably have your own opinion, but expressing it will almost certainly lead to an argument with whoever may be listening.

All these differences are summed up by the fact that the precision and constancy of the logical part of us can be duplicated by a machine, while our emotions can't. Hardly a novel observation. The theme has been with us in literature and folklore since we first started living with science and machines. Most writers have further embellished the basic point with the warning that trifling with this rule can be hazardous to your health. The golem, Frankenstein's monster, robots, and a host of creatures from deep lagoons and careless laboratories have all carried the message that creating things coming too close to life must invite disaster. The unfeeling, soulless machine will always turn on its maker and attempt to destroy him.

I have never understood why machines are always depicted in these stories as being so sinister. Maybe people who understand that don't study engineering. The basic idea, though, is certainly correct. Making machines that look like people or that duplicate parts of human behavior does not mean making living creatures or active brains. And the logic machine obviously comes under the same limitation. But so does logic itself. Neither in the machine nor in the human mind does it represent complete intelligence.

For a closer look at its shortcomings, go back to the question of how we make decisions. What logic can do you have already seen. It can cope only with the detection of a 1 or a 0 appearing on the left side of a numerical answer. From that limitation came the conclusion that we have to look to the nonlogical parts of our thinking to find the mechanisms by which we make most of our decisions. We have to use our emotions and our intuitions.

You undoubtedly have a clear mental picture of what an emotional decision is. It's an impulse, an outburst like, "I'm gonna go in there right now and give that two-faced hypocrite a piece of my mind!" But most of the time our emotional decisions are far less passionate and far more subtle, so subtle that we often don't realize what we're doing.

Take the way engineers make decisions. They are, as a group, justly famous for their precise and mathematical approach to life, and you might expect that if anyone had been able to take the emotions out of decisions, it would be these paragons of logic. You would be right. They have found several ways of doing just that.

Their favorite technique is something called the "figure of merit" or some similar name. It's one of those concepts that can be very useful under the right set of conditions but can get out of hand if you're not careful.

The object of the exercise is to reduce a decision to mathematics, to replace bias by calculation, personal preference by numerical reasoning. In essence, you set up an algebraic equation in which the letters represent the characteristics of the alternatives between which you are trying to choose. You then give numerical values to these characteristics, and when you work out the equations with the assigned numbers, you have reduced each alternative choice to a single number, the figure of merit. It then becomes ridiculously simple to decide which of the alternatives is best—the one with the highest number wins.

The outstanding feature of the system is its orderliness. You have reduced the decision to one that the computer can handle with its strange subtraction. Your decision is logical beyond criticism.

I went through that very quickly, and it glistens very nicely on the surface. But when you look closer, you find a few little flaws in the diamond. Here an example is much more helpful than an abstract discussion, and anybody who has spent some time around engineers can easily come up with one. While the technique is most often used to choose between several possible solutions to a technical problem, many engineers find it irresistibly seductive and use it in the most unlikely situations, to the amazement and amusement of simpler folk, including some other engineers.

The first decision Ben made on the job was a case like that. The day he came to work for us, he appeared without advance notice, carrying an impressive stack of reference documents in his arms. He said nothing to any of us, except to ask which desk he could use. He found one, spread out his papers, lowered his head, and dived in. All morning long he worked without pause. Page after page of calculations came off the end of his pencil. His slide rule glowed hot. His diligence was an awesome sight, an inspiration to us old-timers.

When he showed signs of working through lunch time, I decided to be friendly and break into his creative frenzy. So I walked over to his desk, tapped him on his shoulder, and introduced myself. "Glad to see that you're so deeply involved in your job so quickly."

"Job?" Ben looked at me blankly. "I haven't started on the job. I haven't even met my boss yet."

Puzzled, I gestured at the stack of papers on his desk.

"Oh, that. I'm just figuring out the best way to come to work."

My silence must have told him that I wasn't following the conversation, because he went on to explain. "We've just moved here from New England, and we've rented a house in Westwood. I found out that there are three ways I can get to work from there—the train, the bus, or driving. So I got these maps and timetables together to decide which would be best. Here," he went on with a touch of pride in his voice, "let me show you what I've got so far.

"I've reduced the problem to four variables"—he pawed through the pile of papers, found one, and held it up—"cost per day, which is C in this equation, T for total travel time, D, the distance I would have to walk, and t, how early I would have to get up in the morning. To find F, the figure of merit, I started with the unweighted equation, $F = (t - 6{:}00)/T \times C \times d$. The numerator expresses the fact that I don't want to get up any earlier than 6 A.M., so F goes to zero at that point. You'll recognize, of course, that the factors in the denominator are the ones I want to minimize." He looked at me with a question mark on his face, so I nodded.

He was becoming increasingly enthusiastic. "Here's how the equation worked out. The train leaves our local station at 7:27, so I would have to be up at 6:34, walk 0.4 miles to the train, and another 0.7 miles to the office from the railway station. Total transit time from home to my desk is 26 minutes at a cost of $1.27 per day. That gives a figure of merit of 1.2 for the train. The bus works out to 1.1, and driving gives the best figure, 2.6, primarily because I can sleep the latest and have to walk the least."

Somewhat to my own surprise, I found that I was indeed following the conversation. "Then that's settled, isn't it? You'll be driving."

"No," he said, a bit reluctantly. "My wife won't let me have the car. She doesn't like me to drive in heavy traffic. Besides, I don't like driving, so I'm reworking my figures to see if I can find a way of justifying the train. I really do prefer it."

He had lost me again. "But if you prefer the train, why not simply take the train?"

He looked at me oddly. "You mean just go ahead and take it? Without any rational justification?" I nodded.

"Oh my, no," he said firmly. "It has to be justified. The approach I took was this. Since I expect to spend some of the travel time thinking about my work, I decided to assign a value factor to that, and to crank it into the equation." He dug out another sheet of paper. "So my next step was to take my hourly salary, without overhead, and multiply it by a factor for each mode of travel that expresses the percentage of time it would allow me to think. I put that in the denominator as a decrement of the daily cost and then recomputed. The results came out better, closed the gap a bit, but still didn't quite justify the train. So for my third pass at the problem, I modified the equation by . . ."

I went to lunch by myself. For a long time afterward, the less sensitive souls among us would direct new people to Ben. "Ask him why he takes the train to work." He would always tell them, in all seriousness, "Because I worked out the problem very rigorously and found that the train has the highest figure of merit. Here, let me show you my calculations."

The question now before the house is how Ben really made his decision. Obviously he set a goal based on personal preference and manhandled the equation until it yielded a result that met his goal. The mathematics was a way of showing logically that the best thing to do was the thing he wanted to do from the beginning. His decision was an emotional one.

Emotion plays that same role in many of the decisions we make and in many of the problems we solve. It's the domain in which we set our goals, both at the personal level and at the social level. It's where we make our premises about ourselves and about the people and the society around us.

Those premises—call them goals, aspirations, or expectations if you wish—are the means through which you decide how to set the switches on the AND circuit when you use it for such questions as the decadence of a society. They are the resource you use while the machine sits there with endless patience waiting for you to provide the input which logic and logic machines can manipulate but can never provide for themselves. But we keep muddying the distinction between the assumptions and the logic.

You can lose that distinction without going through Ben's kind of algebraic gyrations. It comes up many times in much more casual surroundings. You will often hear it said that it's logical for people to try to get along with one another. It isn't logical at all. Expressing a desire to live without conflict is an emotional statement. It explains our preference for the kind of world we want. It is an assumption about the people part of the world, made with our feelings, not with logic.

The goals we set for our society can be benevolent or bloodthirsty without any implication that one is more logical than the other. Good logic can lead you to any conclusion about society that you care to name, depending only upon the direction in which your emotions point you. If you start with the assumption that people are divided into races, of which some are superior and some inferior, and that this difference provides the master race with complete power over the lesser, you can proceed to prove that genocide is only an exercise of the valid powers of a society. If you assume that a small group of people has been endowed with the ability to run a society for the benefit of all, it follows that opponents of this group are enemies of the state and that purges and imprisonment are an appropriate remedy. You could start with these assumptions and use your little AND circuit or a full-sized computer to show that your conclusions are logically consistent.

How we establish those goals or premises is a subject I don't care to comment on. It gets you into all kinds of delightful debates about heredity and environment, free will, the responsibilities of the individual and of the society. They're a lot of fun to argue about, but they lie far beyond the limits of my subject. Enough for me is the fact that, by some extremely complicated process, we grow into highly complex individuals with our own ideas about what kind of world we live in.

Regardless of how that complicated process may work, it becomes a two-edged sword. Aside from providing us with new premises upon which we can operate logically, it can also act as a barrier to the entry of new ideas. Emotion is the mechanism through which we reject new assumptions before they get any logical treatment at all. It is the home of our major and minor biases and of the major and minor distortions with which we see the world. It acts as a filter that lets through those ideas we approve of and rejects all others.

To make the point that we repel any idea not in tune with our biases, I will now attempt to sell you a new idea regarding one of the most frequently voiced fears of the computer. If you are at all literate you will be aware that there is considerable apprehension that the computer will reduce us from individuals with names to a digitized mass of numbers. As a consequence, goes the theory, we will be robbed of our liberties, stripped of our freedom. Nonsense. Quite the contrary.

It's true that numbers are much more compatible with computers than are names. They have the obvious advantage that they can be assigned without duplication, and they generally fit better into the world of data processing. As a matter of fact, names get translated into digits anyhow, in order to be manipulated by such operations as the decision subtraction inside the computer; it would be much tidier if they came that way to begin with. So the people who run computers would, indeed, like to have everything, including people, identified by numbers.

But the conclusion that the result would be antagonistic to liberty is quite unfounded. Such digitizing, as a matter of fact, would make us more, rather than less, free. Using numbers instead of names would have some very real advantages from a libertarian point of view. Let me list them for you and see if you are convinced.

1. All ethnic connections would be lost. While names are not a completely reliable guide to national origin, they make excellent starting points for the bigot. Numbers, on the other hand, would provide no clues at all. Nobody would be able to tell who was Irish, Polish, Greek, or whatever. Ethnic jokes would disappear or at least change their targets and lose their sting. Nasty jokes about people whose numbers are divisible by eleven don't seem to be very offensive.

2. Sexual classification would disappear from the name. A string of numbers would give no hint of gender in data banks, job applications, or any other records about people. It puzzles me that the women's liberation movement has not yet objected to the practice of assigning different and identifiable given names to the two sexes. When I see the names Howard G. Brown and Helen G. Brown, I immediately know something about the people that numbers wouldn't tell me.

3. Marital status could also disappear. Or alternatively it could be clarified. For this purpose, one digit in the number could be set aside for the person to use at his/her discretion. With ten possible values, this digit could be much more in-

formative than our present Miss, Mrs., Mr., or Ms. For example, 0 could mean single and happy that way, 1 could mean single but looking, 2 could mean married but looking, and so on, up to 9, meaning none of your business. Think how much more meaningful a simple social ritual like introduction would become.

4. Family connections could optionally be lost or maintained by setting aside a group of digits for arbitrary use by children. For the first time, youngsters would be able to participate in the choice of their own identification, rather than merely acquiring it through the accident of birth or the whims of their parents.

5. The birthday could be made part of the name, freeing from all sorts of embarrassment those of us who can never remember when to send cards.

6. All names would be of equal length, eliminating a basic discrimination against us poor folk who have no middle initial while some privileged fat cats walk around with two or three.

7. It would end one of the major causes of discord between people by totally eliminating the world's most aggravating question, "How do you spell it?"

There you are: seven excellent reasons why the elimination of our current names should be started immediately. With one simple change we eliminate prejudice, sexism, inequality, and a host of other archaic and oppressive practices. Down with the name, up with the digit!

If you still aren't convinced, I can put all those factors into the form of a complicated equation and prove that digitizing names has a much higher figure of merit than our current practice. But I suspect that it would make little difference. You have rejected the idea at the level of your feelings and have no intention of listening to any contrary ideas no matter how logical they may be. With all the problems a name may lead to, you still "like it better" than a string of numbers. So do I.

But you do, at this point, have to score one in favor of logic. Having no ability to judge the premises it is fed, it never rejects an idea simply because it's new or not in keeping with previously ingrained likes or dislikes. Logic and the computer are as incapable of narrow-mindedness as they are of affection. Turning away from new concepts is a strictly human function and is probably one reason some people prefer to live in the world of machines.

Emotion's role as the source of our biases is only one of its many hazards. Of all our ways of thinking, it is the most dangerous when uncontrolled and is, unfortunately, the one most often permitted to become dominant. When it does gain an unchecked mastery, thinking of every kind is replaced by raw chemical reaction, a sad state of affairs that is undoubtedly responsible for the poor esteem in which emotion is held.

Despite its dangers, there is still a strong case for considering emotion a vital part of intelligence. Its role in decision making may be masked and shadowy, but it is there. As the source of the premises with which we figure out our reactions to our social environment, it implies a very important limit on the use of the computer or any other machine. And it has the equally important, though negative, influence of shutting out facts and ideas we don't like. My own opinion is that, whether or not we approve of it, emotion is an essential component of our intelligence.

But don't infer from this defense of the emotional part of thinking that I suggest we break the shackles of logic, throw off the oppressive yoke of the syllogism. My argument is, rather, that we have both, should recognize both, and should use both, each in its proper place. Just as you can't resolve your personal preferences by using mathematics, so you can't solve problems of the physical world with tears or laughter or noble intentions.

Ben was wrong to believe that his personal likes and dislikes had to be dipped in mathematics to be made intellectually palatable. It is just as wrong for the student of the humanities to shrug off the workings of the computer as mere gadgeteering of no interest to a sensitive soul. Emotion may not be orderly and logic may not be likable, but I don't see how either can be denied its place in intelligence.

10

Your Intuition Is Showing

THE first time I was offended by being called intuitive occurred shortly after Rod Zexxy was hired into our marketing department. Actually, of course, he wasn't simply "hired" like an ordinary worker; he was "appointed to a position of major responsibility." His arrival, while there were no trumpeters lining the hallways, was nevertheless something of an occasion in our humdrum lives.

Zexxy came to us with, as they say, impeccable credentials. His schooling included several degrees from all the right universities and election to the most prestigious honor societies. He had already held a series of increasingly responsible jobs with major corporations and was the author of a large number of articles and papers. His assignment was an important one, designed to match his distinguished background. He was to analyze our competitors' machines, try to figure out what they would do next, and guide the specifications of our own new products accordingly.

After he had been with the organization a couple of months he was asked to tell the engineering department about his work, and at the appointed hour we gathered to hear what turned out to be a very professional and impressive presentation. I was so impressed that when the talk was over and the four-color charts were rolled up again, I went to see my boss.

"That man Zexxy," I prophesied, "is going to screw everything up."

My boss reacted by showing a commendable interest in hearing what basis there might be for my conjecture. "What the hell ever gave you such a dumb idea?"

"Zexxy is a technical name-dropper."

"And what, may I ask, is that?"

"Oh, come on, you've met the type. It's someone who's always referring to unimportant papers that were published in obscure journals that no one ever heard of. He tells you how well he knows this guy and that guy working in remote labs. Then he puts on a big act about how stupid you are if you never heard of them. That's a technical name-dropper, and in the end they always screw things up."

"Listen," my boss warned, "he must know what he's doing or else they wouldn't have hired him. And besides, you should only evaluate people on their performance. Don't make snap judgments about them. Be careful, you're being intuitive."

The name-dropper's name dropped out of sight after a few more months, by which time things were pretty well screwed up. By then I also had a different boss, so even the opportunity to gloat was denied me. But having been called intuitive still rankled. I thought I knew what it meant, but I had never been aware that it was something an engineer wasn't supposed to be.

So I tried to find out what intuition is all about. It turned out to be a long and inconclusive search. The first clue I found was a definition in an old dictionary telling me that there used to be a school of philosophy which claimed that ethical principles are learned by intuition. Not much help. Then I tried Bartlett's *Familiar Quotations* to see what wise men have said about it in the past. D. H. Lawrence called it the intelligence that arises out of sex and beauty, the old rascal. Nathaniel Hawthorne said that women's virtues, when they have any, are merely impulsive and intuitive. George Santayana felt pretty much the same way, but he compared the intellectual life of people to bees. The males are the sexually atrophied workers, while the "feminine is a queen, fertile, omnipresent in its brooding industry, but passive and abounding in intuitions without method and passions without justice."

Maybe my boss was right. Intuition seems to be something that nice people don't have, especially not male nice people. On the intellectual spectrum, it appears to lie somewhere between moving your lips when you read and never having heard of Sartre. Give up on Bartlett. We're not after queen bees or sex or beauty. Try the *Britannica*.

The encyclopedia took me on a confused trail, but it did lead somewhere. It said that intuition is an untestable way of predicting the future, that it's either a guess or an unconscious form of inference. Sounds reasonable, but what's inference? Better look it up. Here it is, inference: induction, *q.v.* First I look up *q.v.* and find that it is an abbreviation for the Latin phrase "which see." Back to inference. Inference: induction, look it up. Luckily induction is just a couple of pages ahead of inference, a fairly long entry devoted to explaining several sides of what seems to be a very old argument; trying to explain how we draw general conclusions from particular cases. Most of us never realized it was such a difficult matter, we do it so automatically. When we see enough specific cases of something happening just before something else, we draw a general conclusion and say that if so and so happens, then such and such will always happen.

If you watch babies, you'll find that they spend a lot of their time learning this sort of thing. There is a stage in their growth—for example, when they love to grab hold of something, lean over in their chair, and let go. They notice that when they do let go, the toy or the cup of milk always moves away in the same direction—down. They test as many cases of this new phenomenon as their boredom threshold or their parents' patience will allow, and from these cases they draw a general conclusion which they store away as fact: whenever you let go of something, it goes down.

That's induction. Nothing to it. Even a baby can do it. And the conclusion he draws in this case is quite correct. Or is it? Give him a helium-filled balloon and watch how surprised he is when he lets go. He has encountered a case that doesn't fit his other experience. Does that mean, then, that his conclusion was wrong? Not exactly; practically all the time it's quite correct. The baby, it would seem, has a problem in figuring out how the world works.

We all face pretty much the same dilemma. If you hold up a stone and ask me what would happen if you let go, I'd say that it will fall. Why do I say that? Because it fits my past experience and seems like a reasonable thing to expect.

But the defense that something seems reasonable doesn't impress the more precise thinkers. Scientists, in their search for "reality," are also simply trying to do the same thing as you and I and the baby are—trying to figure out general rules which can explain what they see happening through their senses or their instruments. And their record is not as good as you might have been led to believe.

Their egos have been badly bruised in the past when they accepted arguments or beliefs that seemed reasonable, because those beliefs so often turned out to be dead wrong. In fact, if you checked their batting average over the entire history of science you would probably find that the widely accepted theories were wrong more often than they were right. And most of those theories were quite reasonable.

The history of science has its own junkyard, a trash pile littered with the rusting relics of theories which were once the pride and joy of scientists, but which later were found to be untrue. Look up such items as phlogiston, the luminiferous ether, and the indivisibility of the atom if you have any doubts that induction is a dangerous business.

In an effort to cope with the hazards of induction, scientists finally came up with the scientific method, that systematic approach which has been so successful in discovering and exploiting the workings of the laws of nature. The method prescribes a set of rules and tests that any new idea must pass before it will be seriously considered as science. It requires translation of the idea into mathematical terms. It mandates that all observations be accounted for. It demands experimental testing in some measurable and repeatable way that can be verified by someone else. And it has been successful enough that it is easy to lose track of its purpose.

The scientific method is not a technique for discovering good ideas, but for uncovering bad ones. It does not eliminate induction; it provides a way of checking up on it systematically and rigorously. But science, and mathematics too, move forward, not from the scrutiny and criticism of new ideas, but from the birth of such ideas in creative minds. Creativity is the kind of step that Isaac Newton took when he watched the apocryphal apple fall and said something like, "Well, I'll be damned. It seems as though all bodies in the universe attract each other with a force proportional to the product of their masses, and inversely proportional to the square of the distance between their centers. I wonder why I didn't think of that before?"

How such bright ideas work their way into people's heads is the basic and age-old mystery of induction. How does it happen at all? Why are some people better at it than others? Does it have rules and techniques that can be taught and learned? Is it structured in some way, or is it a totally random, uncontrollable process? Is it just a series of guesses, or is it a complex kind of logic for which we don't yet know the rules?

Those questions never seemed to bother the great scientists or mathematicians. They just went ahead having their infrequent inspirations and sorting out the good ones from the bad. But the puzzle did bother a lot of other people, mostly philosophers and folk like that.

If you care to dig deeper into the subject, get ready for a trip into the depths (or onto the heights) of metaphysics. It will lead to questioning whether every effect must have a cause, whether the universe is structured in some orderly way, and even whether there is any universe at all or just our perception of it. Such names as David Hume, Immanuel Kant, and Henri Poincaré are dropped along the way. Great theories are born, flourish, and die, like generations of fruit flies in a biology lab. Induction, it seems, is an arena in which the heavyweights of philosophy do battle.

Well, that's a long way from casually remarking that Rod Zexxy will screw things up or from watching a baby drop a toy. Such lofty issues are much too far off the path I'm trying to follow, and even the name makes me nervous. Induction has too many associations with science and philosophy, and I want to avoid those. Therefore I choose to call this mode of thinking by its popular name, intuition, which, you may by now have forgotten, is what we started out to define. This undefinable way of thinking is not restricted to science and scientists. It is not the sole preserve of deep thinkers. It is an ability we all have and use constantly in our everyday lives.

Since we never did find the definition we went looking for, we will have to go ahead without it. We'll assume that you intuitively know what intuition is, and if that doesn't make sense to you, you're welcome to seek a definition of your own. But before we start to sing its praises as part of our intelligence, it would be less than fair not to look at some of the reasons that it is so suspect in the eyes of people who pride themselves on being careful thinkers.

If intuition were to be brought before a tribunal of experts in critical thinking, the charge would be something like disorderly conduct. The evidence is mostly circumstantial, but very strong. Consider the case for the prosecution. Item: intuition has no rules. Item: nobody knows how it works. Item: it is inconsistent, in that two people starting from the same set of observations usually come up with different conclusions. Item: it is difficult or impossible to check up on or to reconstruct. I ask you, ladies and gentlemen of the jury, how can anyone with a sense of the rational possibly defend that kind of thinking? How can anyone with a normal regard for clear thinking be expected to take it seriously? The prosecution rests.

The accusation is quite correct. Intuition is guilty on all counts. It is indeed disorderly, disorganized, undisciplined, unruly, and unfathomable. But those charges, true though they may be, are really just misdemeanors which can be shrugged off or explained away. The fact that we don't know how it works isn't really very important. The blood circulated in the human body for countless generations before the process was explained by Sir William Harvey. We remember things without knowing how we do it. We perform many mental and physical functions without having the vaguest idea of how they work. We can't claim that we know more than a fraction of the things our minds and bodies are doing, let alone how they are being done. So why pick on intuition?

The real felony of which intuition alias inference alias induction is guilty is that it is often wrong. It has been the source of dangerous folklore. It has been a road map to scientific dead ends. It has been a most unreliable crutch to lean on.

Oddly enough, however, the fact that it is often wrong seems to be one of its major values. If my reasoning sounds contradictory, look at it this way. Intuition does for us mentally what an advance scout does for a party of explorers hiking through strange territory. He is expected to find a way to get them from where they are now to a place where they haven't been yet.

The only way he can do his job is to follow promising paths. He has no guarantee that any of the trails he tries will lead him to his goal, and most of them indeed turn out to be dead ends. He keeps trying until he finally finds the pass through the mountains or the shallows where the river can be forded. The scout's success or failure is judged by whether or not he finds a suitable path. He is not criticized for being wrong much of the time; that's an integral part of his job.

And so it is with intuition. We use it to probe, to try, to search, to open new vistas and reveal new horizons. It is the way we do our mental experimenting. Out of this searching and testing, this stumbling in and out of mental cul-de-sacs, comes that precious thing called creativity. Where you find the person who dares to send his mind along unknown paths, who accepts the high odds of failure, who is not destroyed by every search that turns out to be futile, there you have the person who is rewarded by the bright idea, the new slant, the fresh insight. You can't create new ideas if you're not as willing as the scout is to be wrong more often than you're right.

A lot of people before me have noticed the similarity. Our language is full of references to it. We continually describe creative thinkers as explorers, as wanderers in uncharted territory, as workers at the frontiers of knowledge. The analogies, even though they have become clichés, are excellent.

Explorers don't do their thing by staying in familiar territory. Innovative thinking doesn't happen when we stay within the bounds of existing premises. Logic, of course, is restricted in exactly that way. You must stay with your premises or you aren't being logical; that's a basic rule and it can't be violated. Intuition has no such constraints. It is free to roam, to wander, and to wonder.

When I compare intuition to an explorer and then define his job as "finding how to get from where he is now to a place where he hasn't been yet," the words may have had a familiar ring. It's almost exactly the same definition as the one for a true problem—trying to figure out how to get where you want to go without knowing exactly where you want to go. The similarity is no mere coincidence, because I know of no accurate distinction between creativity and the ability truly to solve problems. As far as I can tell, they are two neighboring facets of the same gem.

The closeness becomes most evident when you go a step beyond simply solving problems and consider an even greater mystery: discovering that there is a problem waiting to be stated and possibly solved. The ability is a rare one and it has bemused and bewildered the experts who struggle to explain creativity. They would dearly love to know why a few people succeed while most of us either refuse to try or fail when we do. They would pay a high price to anyone who could explain the process through which someone becomes dissatisfied with the currently accepted premises about how things work and sets out to find new and better ones. If you ever stumble across the answer and can reduce it to the kind of logical operations a computer can do, fame and fortune await you. You might even get a computer program named in your honor.

But in addition to its vital part in creativity and problem solving, intuition plays one more role in our thinking which is germane to the subject, and that is its function of bringing order into the multitude of things that we sense and experience. Living minds have an inherent and irrepressible faculty for finding patterns in a jumble of data. During all our waking hours, and perhaps even when we sleep, our senses continually bombard us with information. Sounds, sights, smells, all the signals of our environment, rain down upon us without pause. That we can store and remember any of these is a remarkable achievement. But it is downright astonishing that we can find patterns in this random and endless torrent without trying to, without knowing how we do it, and without being able to keep from doing it.

At its highest level you see this in the ability of a genius like Newton or Einstein to take a few random observations and find in them patterns of cosmic validity. But don't be overpowered by their example: don't conclude that you and I are completely out of the game. While the patterns that most of us find most of the time are far less sweeping and of far less consequence than the law of gravity or the theory of relativity, the ability to find them is no less remarkable.

The family is seated at the table, having supper. The doorbell rings. Everybody looks up and says, in unison, "That must be the paper boy." It is indeed the paper boy. If you ask yourself how you knew, you explain that it's because he always comes around to collect about this time every Thursday evening. But nobody was thinking about the paper boy or remembering that it was Thursday. Yet, when the doorbell rang, a pattern was recognized in a collection of data that you hadn't realized you were acquiring.

Like most things, this natural ability is not always a blessing. It can, if you're not careful, lead to embarrassing situations.

For a while I had a boss named Carl. He was a good man to work for, and the only conflict between us came from his fondness for worrying about little things and my distaste for worrying about even major things. But the potential discord was softened by distance, since his office was a few hundred miles away. Except for a meeting once or twice a month, my contact with him and the rest of his staff was mostly by telephone. One day he called me to check the progress, or lack of it, on one of our more controversial jobs. It was a fairly routine conversation until he asked me, "Do you really think this project is a viable one?"

"Sure it is, Carl," I replied, "and tell Paul that if he doubts it he should come take a look at what we've done so far."

"Hey, how did you know I was talking to Paul about it? He just now left my office."

The answer I gave him was long and rambling and primarily designed to change the subject. But I didn't tell him that for a long time I had been able to figure out who had last spoken to him, back at the head office, by the words he used. Carl didn't realize that he was highly imitative when it came to vocabulary and invariably used whatever cliché he had heard most recently. Since I had long before noticed that "viable" was Paul's favorite word, that "posture" belonged to Abe, "escalate" to John, and "ongoing" to Vito, it wasn't hard to tell who had last been in Carl's office. For several weeks he behaved as though he suspected that I had bugged his office, when the fact was that I had simply, without trying, found a pattern in his behavior.

Nor was it an intellectual feat of impressive proportions. We all know things like that and we find it impossible to know how we know them. Something gets stored away in our memories, with or without our awareness that it has been put there. Something else, at a different time, often in an entirely different context, triggers an awareness that the thing we put away relates to what we are seeing now. Our minds, like jigsaw-puzzle fanatics, are always matching, always testing, endlessly searching for patterns.

The importance of this capability has not been lost on the artificial-intelligence community. For a number of years its members have worked diligently at trying to make a computer recognize patterns. The effort has been restricted primarily to visual patterns, such as printed numbers, because with television or similar techniques such subjects are easily convertible to electrical signals. These attempts are important not only for their theoretical interest but because they have a very high potential practical value. There are obviously an enormous number of things the machine could do if it could be programmed to read automatically such patterns as handwritten words or numbers.

For some specific types of patterns the work has been partially successful, but not impressively so. It succeeds only when the format is highly standardized and carefully designed to be unambiguous, like the special numbers on the bottom of a bank check. But the general problem remains completely intractable, especially when you compare the machine's score with the human ability.

Our intuition recognizes patterns of an incredible vagueness. I don't understand Russian, but I recognize it when I hear it spoken. I suppose that if a group of programmers with enough talent and interest in the problem were to take the time, they could probably program the computer to recognize, if not to understand, Russian. Working with competent linguists, they would identify distinctive phonemes, set up statistical tables of how often sibilants occur in English and plosives in Russian. With amplifiers and band-pass filters they could design and program a system to identify the languages correctly with a confidence level of 98.6 percent or some such impressive number.

But that would be a deliberate and painstaking attack on a specific goal. It would be a typical use of the computer. A problem would have been stated, a solution worked out, and the solution, in the form of the proper computer code, finally fed into the machine. It would differ in no way from any of the other problems the computer is used for.

You and I do the same thing completely involuntarily. I have never made it one of my goals to recognize Russian or to figure out how to do so. It just happens. Intuition is an active element, taking its own initiative, finding its patterns without any premeditation or volition on our part. It is the antithesis of logic, that passive reactor to whatever data it is given.

This aspect of intuition leads us toward the sense in which the word is most popularly used. It describes your thinking when you recognize or feel or know certain things. You have found patterns in vague and undefinable information. Somehow you sense that Pete is not telling you the truth, that Henry's youngster is going to get into serious trouble, that Mary will like the movie you just saw.

We all have this ability, but we don't always use it when we should and often don't trust it when we do use it. Our suspicion is grounded in the same old trouble—unreliability. It turns out that Pete is telling the truth, Henry's youngster grows up to be a person of talent and integrity, Mary hates the movie and gets mad at you for recommending it. After enough such experiences we rediscover what we already knew—this way of thinking is considerably less than perfect.

That, by itself, is almost enough to make most of us feel nervous and uncertain in the presence of our intuitions, and as the final blow along comes the weight of authority to act as the ultimate inhibitor. In the face of the bad reviews it gets from the likes of Hawthorne and Santayana, most of us refuse to take intuition seriously, even when we intuitively know that the experts are wrong. And let me reiterate that I'm not peddling it as the only way anyone should think but merely arguing for recognition of its legitimate place in our arsenal of mental weapons.

In my simpleminded theory of what the brain can do that the computer can't, I see intuition as the area in which the recognition of past patterns creates new assumptions, to be tested in their turn by the rigor of logic. New ideas, new relationships, can come only from this uncertain scout in the world of the unknown. It is the tool we have for breaking out of the sterile, precise grip of logic. The escape is temporary, however, because unless those bright new assumptions can themselves pass the test of logical consistency, they aren't worth much.

How intuition functions remains a mystery, but it certainly seems to be linked with the chaotically messy way we store memories. It is as though we had in our heads one of those old-fashioned junk shops whose aging proprietor claimed he knew exactly where everything was but really didn't.

We seem always to be browsing around in our memories, poking into dusty corners, opening old trunks, rummaging through piles of used observations that orderly and sensible organisms would have discarded as soon as they came in. Every new item that comes into this overcrowded secondhand store is compared with all the old litter and clutter to find out whether there is some link, some relationship, that might be interesting or useful or just plain fun.

Every bit of incoming stuff is scrutinized as by a suspicious pawnbroker. It is turned every which way and carefully examined. Have I seen this kind of thing before? What happened when I saw it? Is there a relationship here? If this part of our intelligence had a coat of arms it would be a question mark rampant on a field of random data.

And you know what? We find a lot of gems in that litter. Some of those questions turn into keys that open doors to new knowledge. It doesn't happen often, but often enough that I have stopped being upset at being called intuitive.

11

The K Vector

YOU already know that I consider technical name-dropping to be something of a vice. But suppose I proceed to do something that I'll call "finding a legitimate place for the introduction of precise terminology with the goal of maximizing the communication of complex concepts at an interdisciplinary level." Surely that would turn an odiously elitist habit into a praiseworthy effort to close the gap between the specialist and the public. It wouldn't be the same as name-dropping, would it?

That is by way of introducing the subject of three-dimensional vectors with independent orthogonal components. If you never heard of those technical wonders, don't be upset. The idea behind vectors is quite simple, and they are not as unknown to you as you may think.

Vectors are an important subject in engineering schools because they are a mathematical tool of basic significance. They are essential to understanding how moving bodies respond to forces, to the calculation of stresses in structures, to the entire theory of electromagnetic effects, including the propagation of radio and light waves. They have all sorts of uses in the technical world because they apply to so many important parts of science.

And according to the theory I now offer for your consideration, vectors also explain the computer as it relates to human intelligence. A vector will be the perch from which the overall view of the computer makes the most sense. It is a simple key for unlocking the puzzle of what the computer can or cannot do, including its potential as a competitor for your job.

You will be familiar with vectors if you've ever been involved with navigation, but even if you haven't come across them before you are certainly familiar with the simplest vector of them all: the location of one place with respect to another. You just haven't thought of it in mathematical terms.

Suppose, for example, that you work in a store 8 miles east and 6 miles north of your home. On a piece of paper make a dot representing your home. Use that dot as the starting point to draw a line due east representing 8 miles on whatever scale you like. From the end of that line draw another line due north, equal to 6 miles on the same scale. The end of that line will locate the store, 8 miles east and 6 miles north of your home. The line directly connecting the point where you started to the point where you finished will slant roughly northeast and will be 10 miles long (trust my arithmetic, or work out the square of the hypotenuse for yourself). That slanting line is the vector, and the east and north lines are its components. If you want to, you can look at it as a way of adding a 6-mile line to an 8-mile line and getting one 10 miles long. At any rate, you have just put together a vector in two dimensions, and the idea can obviously be extended to three dimensions by adding a measure of height.

It is very common in mathematics to start with a concept as basic as northeast and build upon it until you get into theories so lofty and complicated that you lose sight of their humble origins. Vectors are in that category. Although their trail starts at a point as obvious as defining a length and a direction, the heights to which the road can lead are dizzying. My own ability to follow that trail gave out long before the available theorems and generalizations did, but luckily my theory of intelligence needs only a few basic ideas about vectors.

The most fundamental of these is the sense in which the components of a vector are put together. You have formed a sum of two or more things without really combining them. You add a distance north to a distance east and get a new distance and direction, yet the components remain separate entities. They form a sum but they do not mix.

Most important, they can't be substituted for one another. If you don't go far enough east to reach your goal, you can't compensate for it by going farther north. No matter how many lengths of an "east" component you put together, you won't get a vector that has any "north" or "up" in its direction. You can't make any one of the components by using only pieces of a different one.

My theory suggests that intelligence can be viewed in the same way, as a vector in three dimensions. Its first component is logic, the cold, abstract manipulator of whatever premises we may care to feed it. The second is emotion, the complex, highly individual provider of premises about the people part of the world. The third is intuition, the seeker for patterns and the creative but erratic explorer.

To describe an intelligence in terms of the vector, just visualize thinking as a sort of nonphysical movement. Go so far in the direction of logic, turn so far in the direction of emotion, and then go so far in the direction of intuition. The imaginary line running directly from where you started thinking to where you finished is the vector. It has a length and a direction that depend on the components, on how far you "went" in each of the three directions.

Just as the compass points don't lose their identities when combined to make a specific direction, logic, emotion, and intuition are elements which can be combined into intelligence but which never lose their individual identities. Although they all contribute to the total, they remain completely separate and independent. The components of this vector are no more interchangeable than are the compass points. Just as you can't move north by traveling on an east-west line, so you can't arrive at a logical conclusion by using emotional thinking. Neither can you reach an intuitive "destination" no matter how many logical steps you take. Each of the components points in a different direction, comparable to north, east, and up.

Like diseases and features of the moon's landscape, important vectors are usually named by the person who first discovers them. Therefore the vector describing intelligence will henceforth be called the K vector, a name whose derivation I will leave shrouded in mystery. While the K vector, as a way of looking at intelligence, opens the door to a better understanding of the computer, it is necessary first to warn you about the oversimplification that will be taking place before your very eyes.

I've chosen, quite arbitrarily, to categorize intelligence as a three-dimensional vector because this lets you relate the components to north, east, and up, concepts that are familiar from everyday life. But if even this is too abstract, you can illustrate the three dimensions with your hand. Just hold your thumb and first two fingers all at right angles to each other, and you have a model of the components of intelligence. Engineers are taught to do exactly the same thing when they are learning about electrical generators and motors. It's weird to watch a class of soon-to-be-highly-educated adults taking an examination with all of them staring at their fingers in that odd configuration while they try to remember which finger represents current, which one magnetic field, and which one force, and whether the right or the left hand represents generators or motors.

There is nothing in the theory of vectors that limits you to only three components. You can have as many as you want for whatever theory or idea you happen to be interested in. And if you have trouble relating them to the compass points or find it impossible to visualize with your fingers how four or more things can all be at right angles to each other, such trivial problems don't bother mathematicians and theoretical physicists. They talk happily about n-dimensional vectors, where n is any number you care to pick, work out their theorems and differential equations, and even get what they call "important results" without ever worrying about how many fingers they have. (In mathematics an important result is anything that another mathematician might use some day to get yet another important result.)

Certainly human intelligence should be credited with having many more components than the three I've chosen. The complexity and versatility of our thinking processes go far beyond the range of such a simple classification. If intelligence can be described in vector terms at all, it should be an n-dimensional vector, with n a fairly large number. But in order to stay with ideas that can be fairly easily visualized, some simplifying is required.

The simplification I've chosen is to combine a lot of different elements into emotion, and a lot of different elements into intuition, all of which probably should be treated as separate variables. Emotion and intuition, as I've defined them, are loose words, which cover almost boundless territory. But their constituent parts are closely enough associated to suit what is, after all, neither a text on vector calculus nor a treatise on the psychology of intelligence.

When you start to use the K vector as an approach to human thinking, the major handicap to be overcome is the massive prestige that logic has acquired as the only way an intelligent person should think. We pride ourselves on our ability to use the logical component but hide from others, and sometimes from ourselves, our ability to think with the other two.

In fact, we are so apprehensive about being caught using them that we have developed a whole arsenal of devious tricks to make all our mental "movement" look like steps in the logic direction. One very common subterfuge is simply to use a lot of words and phrases that sound logical but aren't. Criticism in the arts is a good example. Critics, for reasons I can't fathom, are too embarrassed to say, "I hate this guy's stuff. It makes me feel crawly." Instead they will use a thousand words that sound like a logical fury but signify nothing.

The same trick is used in many pseudoscientific activities, such as stock market analysis, in which logic is totally irrelevant. I would use some examples of this hilarious art, but if you ever lost money by listening to it you might not appreciate the humor. Actually the stock market is not hard to understand if you look along the proper component of the K vector. To make money at it, all you have to do is arrange for your own manic-depressive cycles to be in step with the national average.

A variation often used to mask the use of the two less acceptable components is choosing names that make things sound logical, even though they really aren't. For example, the law of supply and demand has a beautifully rational ring, recalling Newton's laws of motion and the second law of thermodynamics. It sounds detached, impersonal, and, above all, logical. But it is simply a euphemism for "people are basically greedy," which sounds subjective, judgmental, and nonlogical, and so it is. It is an assumption about people. It may be true, it may be false; that isn't relevant. But, true or false, it's a statement of belief about how people behave, and its origins are emotional. You can use it as a premise upon which to build a very logical theory of how people interact with one another, but the statement itself cannot become a logical one.

I have no expectation that drawing such fine distinctions will have the slightest effect on logic's unassailable reputation. Regardless, let us forge ahead with the picture of intelligence as seen through the K vector. As a first step, look now at the similarities and the differences between two well-known machines, the elevator and the helicopter.

It isn't hard to list the things they have in common. They both mechanize movement, and they can both carry things up and down. The resemblance is remarkable. And if you were the persuasive type, you might be able to start from those shared characteristics and build a case for concluding that the two machines do pretty much the same thing. If you were a bit more enthusiastic you might even argue that the elevator and the helicopter are basically alike, that one works pretty much the same as the other.

But most of us would shrug off the argument as clearly invalid, because the limitations of elevators are so obvious. They can take you up and down as far and as quickly as you please and, in theory, I suppose there is no limit to how high or how fast they can be made to go. But no matter how powerful they might become, their restriction to the vertical component would remain unaltered. Any time you want to move up or down, by all means take an elevator. You couldn't use it, though, to go across town; it isn't designed to carry you there. It is constrained forever to its vertical dimension. The helicopter can also take you up and down as you please, but it can also move you east or west, north or south. It is free to travel in any of the three dimensions, going wherever you please (as long as you don't carry the analogy below ground level). Yes, it is like the elevator, but it is much, much more.

By analogy to the elevator, the computer is a superb way of mechanizing one of the components of your thinking, the logical. Whenever you need to use that part of intelligence, by all means hop on the computer. Don't try to use it, though, for mental "travel" in other directions; it's as restricted to its medium as the elevator is to its shaft. But the human mind, like the helicopter, is not so restrained. It is able to move at will between the components of the K vector. Just as you wouldn't equate the elevator and the helicopter because they can both move vertically, so you mustn't equate the computer and the mind simply because they can both operate logically. The ability to work in more than one dimension is not a trivial difference. It indicates that entirely different mechanisms are at work.

The analogy between the computer and the elevator is one I've tried on some of my friends in the business, who generally accept it only up to a point. Their usual response is: "What you say may be true for the machine itself, but haven't you overlooked the element that the human adds? Aren't you forgetting the program?"

Program is a magic word we've rather glossed over up to now. We really should pay some proper attention to it, because there has always been the hope in some computer circles that the program can one day be so cleverly written that the machine will be able truly to solve problems, answer unexpected questions, and maybe even tell jokes. In short, maybe the program can provide whatever is necessary to transform a collection of copper and silicon into an intelligent machine. The idea is heard often enough to be worth examining.

The question resolves itself into finding out exactly what the program does and, specifically, whether it adds any ingredient that can make it possible for the logic machine to transcend the obvious limitations of its component parts. Is the program like the driver of a car, determining a destination to be reached and setting a course, moment by moment, for getting there? Or is it simply like the ignition key, activating but not directing the vehicle? The answer to the question is to be found, not in abstract speculation, but by going back to look at the only working parts the computer has.

These are, you remember, the electronic equivalents of the little AND circuit and its brethren the OR and the NOT. In the computer those circuits are connected in such a way as to construct a set of instructions, some of which you have already seen. They aren't very mysterious or impressive. Subtract the number in this memory location from the number in that one. If the answer is negative, switch to the instruction in yet another specified memory location. Send the hundred characters starting at a specified memory location to the high-speed printer.

Those instructions are the only tools the programmer has to work with, and their true nature is best seen in terms of the K vector. Built up, as they are, from a large number of the basic circuits, they are equivalent to using a lot of small lines in the logic component to make a longer line. The programmer's tools are complex strings of logic, but still only logic.

In the early days of computers the programmers worked directly with those instructions to accomplish the job they wanted the computer to do, much as the programmer did with the wallpaper problem. Naturally, the real-life problems they faced were far more complex than that simple example, and putting together the machine's roster of instructions to do those jobs turned out to be remarkably difficult.

When you consider that they had to do their programming in the computer's code, it isn't surprising that mistakes were common. If you are in the tenth hour of your working day, it isn't difficult to write 1304 0972 0726 instead of 1304

0927 0726, a small error but one that could lead to a totally botched-up payroll in a factory and a totally unhappy programmer in his boss's office.

As a natural result of such close contact with the working parts of the computer, those early programmers knew the machine in complete detail. They understood its limitations exactly and, most of all, they knew that the instruction codes they were using simply activated those parts of the machine's circuitry associated with the function they wanted the computer to perform. They were putting together long strings of logic, the instructions, to build very long strings of logic, the program.

Their intimate knowledge led, in turn, to a very close rapport with the machine. The names they called it were often imaginative, sometimes hilarious, and always obscene. The people who paid their salaries, however, did not have the same rapport with the machine and had no appreciation for the grace of the language used to address it. So the programmers had to find ways to shorten the time it took to get a program finished and to reduce the kind of errors that added telephone numbers to customers' bills or sent a thousand copies of the same magazine to one person. Almost in desperation they started to figure out ways to use the computer to help them write their programs.

Their efforts eventually grew into what today goes under the generic name of "software," surely one of the most bewildering technical topics of the modern age. Software is mysterious because it is a complex use of the computer, which itself is not exactly the most well-understood machine in history. But even when you come to understand the computer it does not automatically follow that you will understand software. Before you can do that, you must come to grips with its most striking property—its jargon.

Special languages are hardly new, nor are they very rare.

This is an age when all professionals—teachers, engineers, economists, football coaches, astronauts, bureaucrats—feel that of the hundreds of thousands of existing words, none can adequately express their noble thoughts, so they create their own thousands more. As a result, jargon has come to be a natural and predictable companion of any modern specialty.

But until you come into contact with computer software, you have no true appreciation of the glorious heights to which jargon can rise or of how great a barrier it can become to normal human communication. You have to listen with some respect to such a term as "bug inventory" and express a little surprise when you find that it means the long list of errors that have been found in your work. From whatever direction you approach the subject you run into its shield of jargon. Like porcupines raising their quills, software people set up a barrier that defeats all but the most stubborn attempts to find out what the creature behind it looks like.

Oversimplifying considerably, you can categorize all computer programs as being divided into two basic varieties. One is the kind that does the work that the customer bought the machine to do in the first place. These are the programs for running a business, designing a product, doing research on lasers, or calculating the wallpaper needed for your living room. They can be classified under the general heading of "applications programs."

The other kind of programs, the software, are written by specialists to help the applications programmer. They keep track of where items are stored in the memory, provide code words which simplify the use of the basic instructions, keep things organized when the computer is doing more than one job at the same time, and do other tasks of similar nature. They could be compared to kitchen utensils. You can't eat a frying pan or a mixing spoon, but you need them to prepare the meal. In the same way, software programs don't do useful work themselves but are tools to help get the useful work done.

In a relatively short time software became a very big business. Most computer companies now invest more money and manpower in it than they do in engineering the equipment. It has become more and more elaborate, and in the long run it has greatly expanded and simplified the use of computers. But it has also had a less desirable effect. By acting as a buffer against the agonizing attention to detail demanded by the old ways of programming, it has also acted as a blanket covering the reality of what the computer does. Too many computer users today know the machine only through endless layers of the jargon. They are familiar with virtual machines, emulators, macroinstructions, metalanguages, and endless lists of clever acronyms, but not with what the software really is.

In reality the software itself is simply a program, or more accurately a set of programs. These are complex and difficult to understand, intricately woven into a complicated network of interlocking parts, but they are essentially programs, made up of the same basic computer instructions that the programmers previously worked with directly.

Through all the increasing scale of complexity there has been a regular progression. The basic computer circuits were built into long strings of logic, the instructions. These in turn were pieced together to form very long strings of logic, the program, and then extremely long strings, the software. Nowhere along the way has there been any departure from the same elementary logic principle involved in two switches and a light bulb.

So don't be misled by the frightening intricacy of the final product. Remember that no matter how exotic the application may be, no matter how much software is piled on top of software, no matter how elegant the program, at the bottom of the heap it all reduces to three little Boolean operations being done at unbelievable speeds. There is only the capability to mechanize logic. To expect any kind of program to change that fact would be like outfitting an elevator with automatic controls, fancy switches, and sexy lighting and then trying to make it behave like a helicopter.

Just as the constraints on the elevator are inherent in its design, so are the constraints on the computer. It is inherently limited to action in the logical component because that's all its fundamental parts can do. When the individual elements can act in only one of the three dimensions, there is no way you can put them together to step beyond that dimension. No matter how many miles you drive along an east-west road you can't move north.

According to the theory of the K vector, the same holds true for intelligence. No matter how many millions of logic operations you put together, you can't create emotional or intuitive thoughts, you can't produce creativity or intentional humor or new ideas of any kind.

You can't even use bits of logic to make something as fundamental as the question mark. That is a familiar symbol which you have used for so many years that you take it completely for granted. Dig it out of that obscure corner of your mind for a moment and hold it up to the light for a closer look in terms of the K vector.

The symbol represents a seeking beyond what you presently know, a dissatisfaction with the information you already have. It is a perfectly normal human function but would be in complete contradiction to the very nature of logic, which is, at all times, a closed system in which all needed assumptions already exist. You aren't operating in the logic component when you ask a question.

In case that sounds like an exaggeration, test it for yourself. Take a typical question a child might ask, like "What makes a helicopter stay up?" and try to reduce it to a series of AND's, OR's, and NOT's. You'll find that it can't be done, and you'll rediscover that problems and solutions are different and that logic can cope with only one of them.

The logic machine can do only as much as its parent discipline. It can be wired or programmed to perform any logical or mathematical function you might care to dream up, but there is no circuit, no collection of transistors, diodes, or resistors, that can duplicate the question mark. In terms of the K vector, asking a question lies in a component other than logic.

The issue, then, reduces to how you rate the importance of the symbol. Would you make the ability to ask a question one of your criteria for defining intelligence? To the degree that you answer "yes" to that question you have used the K vector to show that there is at least one other dimension of thought that the one-dimensional logic machine can't handle. You have established a limit to what the computer can do.

12

You and the Machine

THE most interesting, if not the most important, use of the K vector is in explaining how the computer relates to you as an individual. It gives you an easy but accurate way to compare the working of your own mind to the operations of the computer and even to calculate exactly how much of your job the machine will ever be able to do.

With all the high-powered research that has been devoted to the subject of how the computer compares to people, the task doesn't seem to be one that can be accomplished in a single chapter of a nontechnical book with an idea as simple as the K vector. But the problem can be brought down to manageable size by reaching into our bulging bag of intellectual tricks and pulling out two very handy mental maneuvers, the well-known fact and the simplifying assumption. Although that devious duo of debate are widely known, experts are nervous about using them, probably because it leaves them open to criticism by their peer group. But we laymen need have no such inhibitions.

The well-known fact is by far the better-known gimmick of the two, and much more commonly used. It is particularly useful when you are more interested in pushing a point of view than in observing good scientific form. In fact, most of the time it can be roughly translated as "Please don't argue with me, just let me make my point." In a heated argument, using a well-known fact has the great advantage that even if it doesn't convince the other guy, it will at least change the subject to just how well known your fact really is.

Like all folk customs, the use of the well-known fact is not as easy as it might appear to the casual observer. It is quite an art to pick a well-known fact obscure enough to take your opponent by surprise but not so far out as to sound like something you just invented.

Citing sources is an equally subtle problem, because well-known facts have a hierarchy all their own. They range in credibility from something you dimly remember reading in a book, to something your barber heard from one of his customers, all the way down to a quotation from a newspaper column. The expert will instinctively select the proper source to carry just enough weight, while leaving a line of retreat to save face by blaming somebody else if his fact is shown to be wrong.

At any rate, I will now invoke the well-known fact that people who do the same kind of work also think and behave in the same way. For every job there is a corresponding kind of mind that can be described in terms of the K vector. This is a fact so obviously true as to need no supporting evidence; your own experience has probably convinced you, just as mine has me.

I have been involved rather closely over the years with people from computer companies in England, France, Germany, and Japan, as well as the United States, and I can attest that like thinks alike. I found among the people I met all the expected differences that came from their varied national backgrounds and cultures. But the differences paled into triviality against the overpowering similarities that went with their work. Their engineers, their salesmen, their production people were all like ours.

Nor is this circumstance restricted to the one industry. Soldiers all around the world understand and respect one another, no matter what their uniforms. Doctors, farmers, wood carvers, policemen, artists, fishermen, chefs, musicians, or members of any other trade or profession form a community of easy understanding that completely transcends national, cultural, or racial boundaries.

The training that people get for and on the job influences the way they think. It may even be the other way around: people who think alike tend to seek the same kind of training and career. Whatever the reason may be, the similarities are there. It is a well-known fact.

But it is an equally well-known fact that all doctors or all machinists do not think exactly alike. Even among the members of any one job group there are limitless variations.

If you were to press me to explain the apparent anomaly, my answer would center around the point that all of us are members of many groups besides our trades. We are parents, voters, drivers, football fans, and on and on. Each of these groups has a way of thinking, a K vector, associated with it. Each of us, then, ends up with a way of thinking that adds together the components of all the groups we belong to. The result is a different combination in each of us of the elements we all have in common.

For the purpose of explaining how you relate to the computer, however, it makes more sense to call upon the second of those forensic foibles, the simplifying assumption. It is less common than the well-known fact, but it is near and dear to the hearts of scientists and engineers, who use it all the time. They have never tried to keep the idea a secret but, on the other hand, they have never made a big public fuss about it either. But I feel that it's useful enough that it shouldn't be restricted to the knowledgeable few, so let me clarify it. You might well want to make it part of your own armory of intellectual weapons.

To start with, you have to tackle a challenging problem, one that nobody before you has been able to solve. You charge in with the greatest confidence and work away for a while, only to realize that the problem is much more complicated than you thought it would be. So you make a simplifying assumption. You hunt for one little piece of the puzzle that you think you can cope with and resolutely ignore the rest. You work exclusively on this one piece and claim that its solution, if you find it, "makes a contribution to our understanding of the total problem." You haven't solved the challenging problem, but you have gotten a paper published.

This may sound like rationalization plus a little self-deception, and it often is just that. But it works remarkably well some of the time, and a lot of difficult and important problems have been solved, piece by little piece, in just that way.

We'll borrow the technique now and carve out for attention only one chunk of the complex problem of human thinking. We'll make the simplifying assumption that the K vector defining the way people think on the job will adequately describe them for the purpose of comparing human intelligence to the computer. (You must understand, though, that I have no intention of doing any more than making a contribution to our understanding of the total problem.)

Before we start to put together K vectors for different people, we have to sharpen our definition of intelligence just to make certain there's no misunderstanding. We will exclude all reflexive behavior. Pulling your hand away from a hot stove, throwing out an arm to keep your balance, sustaining your heartbeat, nothing of that sort will be considered. Our brains and bodies do those jobs by themselves, with no regard for how well or how poorly we think.

We will also exclude the mere accumulation of facts. I happen to know that the principal export of Tibet in 1937 was yak tails. Such knowledge may make me unique among my friends, but it does not make me intelligent. Nobody ever calls a dictionary or an encyclopedia an artificial intelligence. When we find facts on the printed page we recognize them as merely resources with which intelligence can work. We must keep the same distinction when we find them in people.

With that background, the task of putting together somebody's K vector turns out to be quite straightforward. You simply pick the job you are interested in and examine it carefully. Then you decide what percentage of the thinking it demands is logical, what percentage is emotional, and what percentage is intuitive. Those percentages become the components of the K vector.

The key to the problem is to look critically at what people actually do and the kind of thinking it takes to do it. It's vital not to accept gullibly what people would like to have you believe about their work. Remember that logic is much more prestigious than the other two, so people generally like to claim that their days are dedicated to logical thinking.

There are good reasons for working with percentages when comparing different K vectors. We are not concerned with how much intelligence people have, but simply with the proportions of its component parts. We will completely avoid the issue of which people are smarter than which other people and why. Such a debate would be inflammatory, inaccurate, and inconclusive (but it sure would be a lot of fun).

Percentages also have the happy habit of adding up to 100, and that's the nice round number that the components of the K vector will always result in. But while it will simplify the arithmetic and make the theory easier to handle, my years of training force me to confess that we'll be using incorrect mathematics. In reality, the components of a vector aren't summed up by simple addition. But our naive approach will be adequate for the job at hand and will keep us from having to deal with square roots of sums of squares, a benefit for which it is certainly worth trading a little imprecision.

Once you have divided up the intelligence into its three components, focus your attention on the logic part. We could, in fact, forget about the other two, but working them out rounds out the process nicely and at the same time provides an opportunity to gossip about other people.

The significance of the logic percentage is easily seen. Since logic is the only part of your intelligence that you share with the machine, this number becomes the percentage of your job that the computer can do. This doesn't mean that the work is now being done by the machine or that it ever will be done. It represents the theoretical limit of what the machine can do.

To see how the system works, look first at the K vector for the computer. You know by now that the logic machine can perform any function that can be reduced to purely logical steps and absolutely no functions that involve the other two components. So its K vector has to look like this:

L (logic) = 100
E (emotion) = 0
I (intuition) = 0

Remember that the score doesn't measure the intelligence of the machine, it just describes the proportions into which whatever intelligence it may have is divided. It also leads to the startling conclusion that the amount of a computer's thinking that a computer can do is 100 percent.

But that was just a test run, after all, a limbering-up exercise to get ready to deal with people. Before starting, though, a word of caution is in order. The K vectors I've built up for various types of people have no scientific basis on which I care to defend them. They are my own conclusions, based only on hundreds of months of studious, bewildered, fascinated, amused, astonished, and, above all, interested observation. If your experience has led you to different conclusions, I won't argue. My goal is to show you how to use the system for your own purposes, not to convince you that your view of people should be the same as mine.

With that disclaimer, then, follow the reasoning as we build up the K vector for our first specimen, the accountants. They make a good choice to illuminate the process because theirs are the human intelligences easiest to analyze. Remember, we are restricting ourselves to considering the person at work, and not in any other role.

When you look at an accountant's job, the first thing you see is numbers, an endless number of numbers, numbers in rows, in columns, in tables, and in charts. There are numbers in books, numbers on scraps of paper, numbers on adding-machine tapes, numbers everywhere. An ocean of calculation, a sea of arithmetic.

The second thing you see is rules: This number must always be entered in that column. This total must be the same as that one. The numbers in this book must be added up by the second Thursday of every month. It is a world in which consistency and regularity are the primary virtues.

There are good reasons for all this dedication to routine. One certainly hopes that any organization with which one has financial dealings will keep accurate records and not change its system every week. There are also laws which make the accountant's job have the flavor it does.

But for whatever reasons, the outstanding characteristics of the work are immersion in numbers and the pervasive presence of prescribed rules. These belong to the world of logic, so a score of 90 percent for that component of the vector would be about right.

What about emotion? Accountants use it rarely, and when they do, it usually consists of getting mad at other people for not following the same rules with the same single-minded intensity. Mark them low on that one. The use of intuition is equally rare among them, which is not surprising. Remember that intuition is closely linked to creativity, and creativity is not the most outstanding strength of accountants, especially the honest ones. We'll assign a score of 5 percent to each of those two parts.

So the accountant's K vector looks like this;—

$$L = 90$$
$$E = 5$$
$$I = 5$$

Regardless of what other revelations the vector may provide, the size of the logic component shows that 90 percent of the accountant's work can be computerized. The conclusion certainly fits the way things have worked out in practice. Accounts payable, inventory records, payrolls, depreciation tables, all such affairs are natural fodder for the logic machine.

It was for such matters that computers were first used outside of the sphere of science. It is where they are still most widely used in industry, government, education, and so on. An odd result is that in many organizations the computer operation has become part of the financial department, a perfect example of arriving at a logical but foolish conclusion.

That profession was easy, so move up the scale for a closer look at a considerably more complex job, the executive's. Here you have a profession that has been the subject of ever-increasing analysis and scrutiny, starting from the time that we humans first banded together into groups to accomplish some common end. Interest in the people holding the executive's job has reached its peak in this age of the big organization, and they have been probed and examined by everybody who can spell the word.

Popular books are written, doctoral dissertations are dissertated, and consultants fly around the country offering sage advice on the care and feeding of the executive. Careers and fortunes are made on the promise that people can be taught the skills, habits, and attitudes needed to qualify for one of these lofty jobs. That isn't my goal. Enough for me is a comment or two about the K vector that goes with this so highly regarded job.

The person under scrutiny is an executive in any medium-to-large organization. It could be an industry, the military, government, a university, a church—it doesn't matter. An executive is the same kind of person wherever he or she may be employed. Moreover, we are interested only in the people who actually learn how to do the executive's job. We're not concerned with accountants or engineers or others who are promoted to executive rank but don't have the right thinking components. Their records as executives are universally disastrous.

The executive is also an excellent example of a case in which one should not be deceived by public images. Executives portray themselves as highly logical. They have built a convincing picture of people who spend their time weighing facts, listening carefully to rational opinions, and arriving at coolly and logically calculated decisions. In reality, of course, that's not what executives do; it's what some of the people who work for them do.

You find the misconception cropping up in all kinds of ways. In a plant where I once worked, a firm of decorators was brought in to renovate the executive offices. One day I wandered into the area, popularly called the Forbidden City, to see how the work was progressing and to offer my usual helpful suggestions.

I found the work crew putting the finishing touches to a set of rooms that gave the impression of being invisible. The walls and carpet were light tan, the furniture was light tan, and the draperies were light tan. The walls were hung with carefully selected prints, all of them soft abstracts in pale greens, pale blues, and pale tans. The only bright color in the room came from a red-handled screwdriver someone had left on a chair.

"Ye gods! Why so bland? It looks like the inside of a custard pudding."

The answer I got was very chilly. "The decorator feels that executives require an environment totally conducive to thinking. It should be unobtrusive and calm and have no disruptive design elements."

Somehow that statement didn't conform to my own experience. So, to check out the idea that an ambience of monastic contemplation was best suited to executives, I organized a small task force to conduct an unscientific poll among the people who would work for the men occupying those offices. "How would you decorate your boss's office to suit best the way he works?" was the question.

When the results were compiled, my suspicions were confirmed. We first discarded those suggestions that reflected, not the boss's working technique, but his personality, regrettably eliminating such excellent decorating motifs as a cobra's wicker basket or a whore's bedroom. Still, when we analyzed those that remained, the poll resulted in a remarkable consensus. The offices should look like the bridge of the *Titanic* when it hit the iceberg. The employees knew their bosses better than the decorator did.

In reality, executives see peace, quiet, and deliberate thought as unhealthy symptoms of decadence, incompetence, and, worst of all, an academic approach to life. To stave off these dread diseases, they surround themselves with ringing telephones, dictating machines, buzzers, and voices. Activity and commotion are their nutrients, their vitamin pills.

If you happen to walk into an executive's office and catch him thinking, he will invariably be highly embarrassed. He will quickly explain that he isn't just sitting there thinking, he is waiting impatiently for an important call from Brussels, or his damned secretary is late finishing some vital papers he will need for the meeting of the Planning Committee that A.D. just called, making him reschedule six other meetings and not get home until eleven o'clock tonight. Executive folkways call for frenzy on the job, not deliberation. Even when they do admit to having spent some time thinking, they will invariably claim that it was either at home on a weekend or in the middle of the night when less dedicated people were idling away the hours in leisure or sleep.

If you brush past the public image, ignore the hubbub, and take an unbiased look at the kind of minds executives have, your first observation will be a large chunk of emotion. Don't be surprised to find it in these supposedly implacable men. Strong ambition is an emotion, and it is certainly a universal characteristic of these people. Why else would anyone want the job in the first place? Stubborn determination is also there in abundance because, with the exception of a few hereditary positions, the top spots in any organization are not won by the casual player in the game of influence. These elements are so necessary to the executive that if your emotional makeup doesn't include a healthy appetite for authority, forget about the job. You'll rarely get it and if by some chance you do, you won't be very good at it. These feelings are important enough to justify giving the emotion component of the executive's job a score of 35 percent.

Then look, with the same disregard for puffery, at the work that an executive actually does for a living. You'll find that it falls into two broad categories. First, he must work with people. He must select, instruct, and supervise groups of them to reach a set of goals. He doesn't have to have a lot of empathy, or to relate to other people emotionally, or even to like them very much. But he must understand them as individuals and as groups. People are the means through which he does his job. They are the tools of his trade, and, as with any craftsman, the success of his work depends on how well he has mastered the use of his tools.

His skill, or lack of it, in this category is most severely tested when he has to judge the potential performance of people in situations they have never faced before. When the time comes to hire, to promote, or to assign new responsibilities, when a decision must be made on selecting the right person for the right job, you can start to sort out the good executives from the poor ones.

George, the office sage who had earlier put psychologists into perspective for me, was also the one who made me understand this part of the executive's job.

"George," I once remarked, "that Notthead is the dumbest guy I've ever seen behind a general manager's desk. I wonder why they don't fire him."

"That doesn't bother me," he said after his usual gloomy pause, "but the big wheel who hired Notthead, he's the one who should be fired before he has a chance to make any more swell choices like that one."

As usual, he was right. The guy who had hired Notthead finally fired him but made an equally poor choice the next time. Not surprisingly, things got even worse than they had been before. And if you dig into a random selection of organizational catastrophes you'll find the same basic theme coming up time and time again: the wrong person being assigned to the wrong job.

Choosing whom to trust to do what is clearly not the kind of decision you can make by subtracting one number from another. You learn to judge people and to predict their potential only by watching them over a period of time and finding relationships which you often can't even explain to yourself. You put together a picture that integrates all the data you have absorbed consciously or unconsciously. You predict how people will perform in new situations by absorbing patterns of behavior at the intuitive level.

It is an uncertain process. The chance of error is high, there is no assurance that any conclusion you may reach is correct, and no one is right all the time. But there is no other way. There are no simple formulas, no magic wands. It all comes down to "insight," whatever that may be, and the executive who does this part of his work poorly is in serious trouble, and so is his organization.

In the second broad division of his job, the executive must always be looking ahead in time. He is constantly called upon to foresee the results of taking this path or that one, of making a selection between several alternative courses, each of them with unprovable consequences. The decisions he faces concern what might happen in the future as the result of some action he may take, or not take, today. Will there still be a market for left-handed frying pans by the time we build the new factory? Is this the time to extend the new subway? If we start a church building fund now, will the congregation be willing and able to raise the money? He is continually expected to deal, not with yesterday or today, but with tomorrow.

In the innocent old days, such work was called prophecy and was associated with magic and occult powers and mysterious cosmic forces. Such trappings are, by their very nature, repugnant to the modern, rational man and especially to the hard-headed businessman. How could he possibly live with the realization that a major part of his work traces back to such luminaries as the Delphic oracle and the guy who wandered around saying, "Beware the Ides of March"?

So prophecy has been abolished. The executive discards all the old mumbo jumbo and calls upon the most modern systematic techniques. He doesn't prophesy, he makes forecasts. He doesn't consult the stars, he makes cost-effectiveness studies, conducts market research, and even dabbles with mathematical systems like operations research. He calls upon the skills of statisticians, psychologists, economists, accountants, product specialists, and systems analysts. He gathers around him the finest products of modern technology, education, and research to help him in his task.

But it still all boils down to prophecy. Changing the name or changing the tools can't alter the fact that trying to look into human affairs beyond this instant on the clock casts you in the role, not of the logician, but of the explorer. You are trying to set a course without knowing for sure where it is that you are going.

The successful executive recognizes that fact. He'll use all the modern tools he can find to help point the way, but he recognizes that in the end he must depend on his own intuitive reactions. That understanding is best seen in the great entrepreneurs of business, men who built industries without much solid support for the idea that a need and a market were waiting out there for the product they had found. And while the average executive doesn't come up to those high standards, it's clear that in evaluating his job we're going to want to score him high in intuition—say 50 percent.

Having worked out the emotion and intuition components, we get the logic percentage by figuring out what's left over. So when we put together the pieces, we end up with a K vector that looks like this:

L = 15
E = 35
I = 50

These figures predict that only 15 percent of an executive's job can be done by a computer. And this, indeed, is one of the areas in which the early dreams of what the machine could do have been least realized. It was anticipated by many early computer people that much of the manager's work would be done electronically. With the apparent ability to mechanize decision-making, some even prophesied that most of the duties of middle management would be turned over to the computer and the people could be largely dispensed with. It didn't happen, and now you know why.

The reason isn't that the problems the executive deals with are so complicated. They are certainly no more complex than many of the mathematical monstrosities that run routinely on the computer in an average university. The failure to computerize the executive's work is due to the fact that so little of it is in the logic component.

Don't draw the conclusion, however, that executives are not capable of logical thinking. I'm sure that some of them are, but since not much logic is required in their jobs, they get out of practice. They will often claim that they are being logical when they are really being cautious, callous, or calculating. These attributes, of course, belong in the emotional component, but because they are cold and unlikable they tend to be confused with logic.

The confusion is not uncommon. Many kinds of thinking are called logical when they really aren't, which serves to underline the care you must use when you undertake to assemble the K vector for a job. It also reinforces the caution that, while the idea can obviously be applied to any profession, you must remember that you can only use the system when you know what the people really do in their work, not what they claim to do or what you may have heard they do. If you don't have that knowledge, your results will be invalid and you would be well advised to stay away from the problem.

Economists, for instance, have always interested me, but I can't put together a vector for them because I don't know what they do. I can't believe that they spend all their time proving mathematically that people would rather make money than lose it. There must be more substance to their job than I can see. But I've never tried to find out what it is, because they seem to be a relatively harmless lot, who become dangerous only when they start to believe that they should be taken seriously.

There is one profession, though, whose work we all observe and on which we are all qualified to comment—that of the politician, toiling away at the critical job of deciding what laws and regulations will be used to make society function the way most of us want it to. It's an important job, well worth a quick look. It's another job that you have to be careful about, because of its strong public image. In this case the image is variable, depending on what your own experience with politicians has been. So, with due recognition of the difficulty of being impartial, we'll forge ahead with the derivation of their K vector.

First, for the logic component. Well, what about it? Beyond whatever deductive ability may be required for basic literacy, the job makes no demands. What problems would a state legislator or a congressman ever come across that would be amenable to solution by logical or mathematical analysis? If you were given enough time and resources, you might find an example, but you would have to dig very deep indeed. As a matter of fact, when I look around the area where I live and observe the chaotic state of the road system, I begin to suspect that even an engineer, when he goes to work for a government highway department, loses his grip on these abilities. Association with a political body seems to atrophy the power of logical thinking. Like the vermiform appendix, it becomes unnecessary for survival, shrivels from disuse, and can even be completely excised with no ill effects. A score of 5 percent for a politician's logic would be adequate and probably generous.

As for emotion, I have to rate politicians unusually high

in that category. Like the executives, they obviously have strong drives for positions of power, but they also have something else. In the general public view, they are often pictured as people who are subject to strong tides of emotion. They are seen as people who get swept away as a body in some highly excitable situation and pass laws or issue edicts on the crest of an emotional wave. While that unquestionably happens once in a while, I don't believe their thinking is generally based on such a reaction. I see them, rather, as people who are very sensitive to the emotions of others, very good at gauging reactions. They tend to be very much aware of other people's feelings and fears and are not above manipulating these to their own advantage. But they always seem to be somewhat detached themselves, measuring and observing but withholding their own feelings, rarely letting their emotions override what seems to be a constant air of careful observation. With this combination, we have to score them at least 55 percent for emotion.

The remaining 40 percent of their intelligence, then, is intuition. But even here the emphasis is on dealing with people. While politicians have a great ability to look ahead to the consequences of their work, it is not in terms of judging whether their actions will advance or retard the goals they are charged with meeting. Instead, their intuitions are strong at forecasting how acceptable their actions will be to their constituents. The result is that they develop a strong sense of what can or cannot be accomplished, rather than of what should or should not be done.

When you put it all together, you have a K vector that looks like this.

L = 5
E = 55
I = 40

The results predict that a very small amount, only 5 percent, of a politician's work can be done by a computer. And, in fact, I know of a very few uses for the machines that have yet been found in this area. Some legislatures use computers to count the ayes and nays during voting and to display the results. There are also a few places where computers are used to keep track of the status of proposed laws in an effort to speed them up as they limp from one stage to the next in their long climb to enactment. But this is clerical work, peripheral to the job itself.

There is one significant part of the politician's duties where the use of the computer, while possible, is notably absent. He deals with matters involving numbers and arithmetic and, more specifically, money. But establishing government budgets is, to say the least, not a rigorous science. Computers won't be any help until the levying of taxes and the spending of revenues become problems in logic. Would you care to guess when that might come about?

There you have the system. You may not be impressed by it, you may not believe it to have any relevance to your own job, you may even refuse to accept it as a general approach to the people-computer relationship. But you must agree that it is a genuinely pseudoscientific way to get some insight into how the computer fits into whatever it is you do for a living.

If you are interested in predicting, for your own amusement, how much of your work can ever be turned over to the computer, you should now find it easy to figure out your own K vector. Just look honestly at all the thinking that your job requires and divide it into three parts. The part demanding the exercise of good reasoning from given assumptions or the unquestioning following of prestated rules, mark down as L for logic. The part requiring the exercise of feeling, either an outright expression of your own or coping with and understanding other people's, mark down as E, emotion. The part calling for establishing patterns between apparently unrelated observations, asking new questions, creating new suppositions which can later be tested logically, label as I, intuition. When the exercise is finished, the answer becomes obvious.

Should you ever try it, you may find yourself in something of a quandary when it comes to estimating the logic component. If you mark your job low in logic, you must come to grips with the reverence we all hold for that exalted component and must decide whether you are ready to confess that you may not have as much need for logic as you might want to claim. On the other hand, if you mark your job high in logic, you will have to admit that most of it can be done by the machine. Have fun.

13

Think Well Before Using

ONCE you start to look at the computer in terms of its restriction to a single component of the K vector, you are able to explain its most spectacular successes and its best-known failures. For such a task as guiding a rocket to the moon, the logic machine is the perfect instrument. The unfailing consistency and precision of the old equations are ideally matched to what the computer can do. The same holds true whenever a mathematical expression can be written to describe precisely how something works. Putting numerical values into equations and calculating the result lies wholly within the logic component.

But just because something is in the form of an equation doesn't mean it's right. The computer can process, with speed and precision, any equation you care to feed it, but before you take the computer's results seriously you had better make very sure that the equation it was given to work on is itself worth taking seriously.

Equations are the aristocracy of the intellectual world. A collection of *x*'s and *y*'s carries with it an aura of profundity and correctness that almost demands our respect, and the more complicated it looks, the more profound and correct we tend to feel it must be. This is probably because we see the basic equations of the physical sciences as so right and so powerful that we naturally attribute the same virtues to equations in general.

You never find that attitude among scientific experts who know just how much disagreement there can be about whether a specific equation is worth looking at twice. Sometimes the battle is fierce and nasty, often involving the giant names of science. When Einstein dared to modify Newton's masterwork he was subjected to a torrent of abuse, criticism, and disbelief. Einstein, in turn, fought bitterly against the implications of some of the equations of atomic physics and never did come to accept them, even though they seem to work. The same kinds of argument go on all the time at all levels in most branches of science.

Writing a new idea with an equals sign in the middle is not, by itself, enough to make the experts accept it. They realize that a new equation is really nothing more than an expression of personal opinion. Only after it has been tested and verified over and over again is it entered into the list of equations that are correct and useful.

You should learn to share some of that skepticism. You probably don't much care whether the speed of light is truly a universal constant or whether there must be uncertainty in measuring the momentum of an electron, nor should the nonexpert get involved in those arguments. There are, however, other equations commonly fed into computers which warrant a quizzical look and a raised eyebrow.

These are primarily equations dealing with people matters, equations written to analyze how our social mechanisms work and to project how they should work. There are many such applications, with more appearing all the time. It has become a popular pastime among mathematicians, economists, and social scientists to do something called "modeling" some aspect of society.

Modeling, in this relatively new context, has nothing to do with posing for a camera or making toy airplanes, but, as modern jargon goes, it's a rather well-chosen word. It actually does provide the researcher with a little universe that he can control and modify at will, just as a model railroader can switch his trains, eliminate tunnels, and move bridges to suit his whim.

Instead of working with miniature depots or toy trees, the computer modeler handles mathematical symbols. What he does bears a strong resemblance, though on a much grander scale, to what Ben did when he calculated the figures of merit for his choices of how to get to work. Where Ben's tools were bus and train schedules, the computer modeler deals with such sweeping topics as a nation's economy, a city's transportation system, or the world's food supply. But the essentials of the job are still similar to Ben's. He examines his chosen subject, decides what the important factors are, and figures out how they relate to one another. Finally he expresses his ideas as an equation which, more or less to his satisfaction, describes how the system functions.

If you could read his mind as he works, you might get something like this: "I'll let *C* be millions of dollars of capital invested in new plant and use the Harvard estimate that each million dollars of capital creates 30 new jobs. So if *U* is the percentage of unemployment in a population, P, I have equilibrium when $C = U \times P/30$. When I crank that into Schultz's equation for capital investment as a function of interest rates and combine it with my own equation for population growth as a function of available jobs, I get so on and so on and so on."

His final result may look to you like an ordinary run-of-the-mill incomprehensible equation, but to the economist who wrote it, it is something else. In his view he has "built" a little world in which all the elements interact with one another in conformance to his own specifications. It is his version, mathematically expressed, of how a piece of society operates.

All well and good, but this kind of thing could have been done at any time and any place, even if the computer had never been invented. All we've used so far is one human mind, a pencil, and some paper. It's the sort of intellectual exercise that Plato might have enjoyed if he had had the benefit of later mathematics. Where does the computer come into the picture?

As usual, what the machine adds to the recipe is simply its speed of calculation. Societies are very complex, and even the most rudimentary mathematical representation of them must also be complex, so much so that plowing through the arithmetic with the old tools was totally impractical.

The computer changed all that. The researcher can now put the equation—his model—into the machine and suddenly have a mythical world whose fate he totally controls. By changing the values of the variables in his equation he can literally change the state of his world, and the computer will work out the consequences. He can make welfare costs increase, drop, or level off and calculate what will happen to the average family size in his model of a city. He can command global population to increase at any rate he chooses to postulate and find out what will happen, in his model of the world, to the earth's supply of oxygen. The power he has is limited only by his skill and imagination.

While it is probably fun to do, there are some legitimate questions. The most basic one is how good the model is. How closely do the equations match the reality of the situation under study? Does the world really work the way the modeler says it does? Nobody really knows, but if you're skeptical you're probably right. No matter how complicated his equation, he still hasn't accounted for all the ways in which the many components of a society interact.

Most modelers are quite aware of the problem and are careful to point out that their models are a gross oversimplification of the real world. They frequently soften their conclusions with words like: "Although it is not possible at this time to show that our model correlates strongly with past experience, the findings presented here suggest that future research could well be dedicated to clarifying those factors which we have identified as not being presently reducible to sufficiently definitive terms."

Their praiseworthy caution, however, often gets lost during the processing of their press releases. Too often their public pronouncements give the impression that the computer has been approached like an oracle by its priestly attendants. It has reverently and ceremoniously been asked a question beyond the grasp of mere human minds. It has reached deep into its own mysterious resources, cogitated, deliberated, and finally spoken in its strange tongue to tell us what our fate will be.

You now know, of course, that the answer to the problem was developed before the computer was even turned on, that running the equations through the machine merely worked out the consequences of the ideas with which the man started. The computer's sole function is to translate the mathematical symbols into a set of specific numbers, carried to as many decimal places of precision as you care to use. It adds no more intelligence to the equations it is processing than an oven adds to the recipe of the cake it is baking.

Once again, the K vector helps you see why this should be so. The computer can work out the numerical results of the equation; that task lies in the logic component. But what comes out of the computer can be no more impartial or intelligent than the assumptions that went in. Underlying the whole exercise are the feelings and intuitions of the person who wrote the equations. No matter how objective a job he may try to do, the subjective can never be entirely eliminated because there is no other source for the premises he needs.

Much of my own suspicion of computer models is founded on an odd set of coincidences. I have noticed that, with very rare exceptions, the computer's results always tend to support the ideas or outlook of the person who "built the model." An economist who favors higher taxes always seems to get the computer to agree with him, to say that, yes, higher taxes would certainly fix things up in a hurry. The next day along comes another economist who favors lower taxes. He puts his model into the same machine, and amazingly the results say that he's right too. It is all a greatly complicated version of the game you and your neighbor played when you set the switches to decide whether the U.S.A. is decadent. In every case the computer tells you exactly what you told it to tell you.

If I appear to be just another engineer picking on the poor old social sciences, let me reassure you that the physical sciences are also full of examples of the perils of computer modeling. You find them wherever the systems under study are complex enough and new enough to be poorly understood, systems that are waiting for someone to have the flash of insight required to put together a coherent package that can be tested and proven. Until that happens, there is only a wide range of educated guesses to choose from.

A case in point is the research in weather and the variables that affect it. The problem here is an unbelievably complex one, in which no one even knows whether all the important factors have yet been identified. When there is agreement on how parts of the weather system work, the equations are so complicated that even the very largest and fastest computers can barely cope with them. As a result, many researchers have turned to various simplified models, some of which prove that a new ice age is definitely coming soon, and others show that it definitely isn't.

The recent turmoil about the effects of aerosols is another fine example. The chemistry involved in the problem is not easily subject to duplication in a laboratory, so both sides have written up their opinions in the form of equations and put them through the computer. The result is thoroughly predictable, with the anti-aerosol forces waving the computer print-outs which prove that the upper ozone layer is under grave attack and the anti-anti-aerosol scientists grinning with delight as the computer reports that nothing of the sort is happening.

Without doubt one side or the other is right, but which? Very simple. Believe the guy whose equations are sound and correct. When the equations are legitimate, so is the result that comes out of the computer. But what if you can't tell whose equations are the good ones? Then by all means believe whichever side strikes the most responsive chord in your own feelings, that most closely reflects your own prejudgments. If that doesn't settle it for you, ally yourself with whoever shouts the loudest or looks most sincere or has the prettiest blue eyes. As a last resort you can always believe neither side until one or the other can prove it is right.

But don't look to the computer for the answer. All it can do is process what it is given, complete with built-in biases and untested premises. A personal opinion that has been fed into a computer comes out the other end as a personal opinion that has come through a computer.

So whenever you see a claim that the computer has figured out how the economy works or how a city government should be reorganized, or prophesied that the world will starve to death next Thursday at 7:27 A.M. local time or that Chile and Norway will soon be at war, you will know what you have to do. Ignore the computer output until you have checked the assumptions that the programmer started with. If you agree with them, then by all means go ahead and read what the computer printed; it will fortify the beliefs you already have. If you disagree with the programmer's ideas, leave the poor old computer alone and go argue with the programmer.

Modeling, despite all its problems, is a legitimate use of the computer. It becomes a source of misconception or fraud only to the degree that someone pretends that the machine has done more than it really has. But modeling is still the processing of a set of equations, the very kind of thing which the machine was always intended to do. There are, however, other uses of the computer which can be categorized only as noble attempts to take the machine beyond the confines of the logic component—with, as you might expect, predictable results. Language translation is a good example.

The problem was tackled early in the life of computers, when enthusiasm ran high and everything seemed possible. The potential value of translating from, say, Russian to English at electronic speeds is clearly very high, and a great deal of talent and money has been applied to the task. But for almost twenty years success has been elusive and limited.

The result of all the work to date is that the computer has found a restricted use for translation in some technical fields, where the vocabulary is well defined and the context is known and narrow. Even here, though, human editing is almost always brought in to make the output readable. For translating general conversational language, the computer has been the source of more funny stories than of useful documents.

The failure makes sense when you consider the challenge of translation in terms of the K vector. On the surface it may look like a difficult but not impossible problem. After all, the most basic ingredient of language is structure. While there is an enormous diversity among human tongues, they all have some fundamentals in common. To make any language useful, words must be assigned agreed-upon meanings and a set of rules must be established for putting the words together. Once you have set up the lexicon and the grammar, you have the elements of a system through which complex thoughts can be stated by one mind and understood by another.

Since rules and definitions are the very kinds of things we tend to associate with logic, it's natural to assume that the computer can be used to transform the mechanics of one language into those of another. And to the degree that a language sticks to its theoretical description, computer translation is quite practical. Where the rules and the vocabulary are truly regular, as in constructing the names of complex chemicals or in medical terminology, the computer can achieve a fair amount of success.

In reality, of course, human communication is never as nice and orderly as the relatively artificial languages of scientific specialties. The structural rules, especially in English, are not very precise, nor are they by any means inviolable. For example, the order in which words are used is sometimes crucial to the meaning, sometimes it's irrelevant, sometimes poetic.

Grammar, on the whole, is as much a point of departure for individual style as it is a rigid mold. People can break the rules to an impressive degree without seriously affecting understanding. It may set my teeth on edge to hear someone ask, "Where was youse at yestiddy?" but I know what he means. Rules that can be followed or broken at the will of the speaker may be fine with people, but a logical system is in serious trouble when it tries to cope with them. There might as well be no rules at all.

While the poorly defined structure of languages causes problems in machine translation, these pale into insignificance when compared to the ultimate frustration of dealing with the words. To recognize how difficult it is to pin down a logical statement for the meaning of even the most basic vocabulary, you don't have to get involved with translation; you can find plenty of examples within the confines of a single language. Here, for instance, are two statements that mean the same thing: "The sun is coming up" and "The morn in russet mantle clad walks o'er the dew of yon high eastern hill." Try, on a word-by-word basis, to work out correct definitions to show that the colloquial and the poetic versions are equivalent.

The problem is compounded, of course, when you try to go from one language to another. You discover that a language is far more than a phrase book; it is the summary of a culture. Even the simplest words are more than mere entries in a glossary. True, they carry meanings which can, with varying precision, be matched against the words in a second language, but it's a very unscientific operation, full of uncertainty, never more than an approximation. Nobody knows how a human interpreter decides which words in one language best correspond to the words in another, but I don't see how those decisions could be expressed as a series of subtractions.

A language, as a vehicle for transmitting thoughts from one mind to another, includes all the components of the K vector. Words and their usage do more than carry ill-defined meanings. They enflame, pacify, irritate, or befriend. They draw pictures, recall associations, trigger new ideas, evoke laughter. All these and similar functions lie in the nonlogical components of intelligence. None of them is within the powers of a computer or of any logical system.

Once you get the feel of it, the K vector can be used with confidence to sort out the practical uses of the computer from the impractical, but be careful. Verifying that what you want to do is in harmony with the computer's capability doesn't, by itself, guarantee success at doing it. For example, how often has a letter like this gone forth from the office of an unhappy company official?

> Dear Customer,
>
> We deeply regret any inconvenience you may have been caused by the errors in your last statement. We have recently installed a new automatic data processing system and have encountered the normal number of difficulties in converting from our previous methods.
>
> We are working diligently to perfect the new system and are confident that, when fully operational, it will provide you with faster and better service. In the meantime please discard all correspondence we have sent during the past month, including any past due notices which may have preceded the mailing of your bill. We will shortly be sending you a corrected statement.
>
> *The Management*

Why so much trouble? Inventory, payroll, billing—the routine aspects of any business—are all structured; all involve relatively modest arithmetic; all are totally reducible to logical steps. In terms of the K vector it should have been easy to do all those things on the computer. It wasn't easy, though, as many will be glad to testify.

The K vector has its limitations, like a blood test that can tell if you're diabetic but can't determine whether you're fit to play football. When dealing with the computer you must continue to keep in mind the misconceptions, the mythology, which, K vector or no, can devastate you if you're not careful. In fact, most of the fiascos with computers in business have originated with that persistent demon, the confusion between problems and solutions.

To many first-time users of computers the distinction came as a severe shock, if, indeed, they ever did realize that it was the root of the trouble. I have never been able to understand precisely what they thought the computer could do. Some of them actually seemed to expect that they could approach the machine and say, "Straighten out the mess in accounts receivable, and when you're through with that, there are some problems over in payroll that I want you to take a look at." They behaved as though they expected to be able to push a button and, presto, the disorganization and chaos in their offices would be replaced by order and structure.

They found, alas, that in a disorganized environment a computer contributed even more and greater confusion. When programmed to do the wrong things, it was far superior to even the most diligent and conscientious human incompetent in its ability to churn out misinformation. Nothing was wrong with the computer; the trouble was that the management had not solved its problems before trying to use the machine.

Those companies that didn't break under the impact of such disasters discovered beneficial side effects. They were forced to study in detail just exactly what they wanted done and how they wanted to do it, and many companies discovered that they didn't have a systematic approach to such fundamentals as billing or inventory control. Trying to use a computer made them face and solve their problems.

There was a variation on this basic theme. Many companies which had carefully planned their methods and procedures programmed the computer to reflect these exactly. Everything was put into the machine "according to the book." The management didn't know, though, that things had been running smoothly, not because of the book, but in spite of it.

Consider the case of Isaac Eyeshade, a quiet little man who used to live a few houses away from me. He had for many years worked diligently and happily at his clerical duties in a large manufacturing company which had sales branches scattered all over the country. As companies will do, Isaac's firm decided to install a computer system which would, among other things, process automatically the orders received from the outlying offices.

The people in charge of the changeover to the computer duly noted that Isaac's job was to review the order forms as they came in from the branches and did a careful study of the situation. The paperwork was found to be well standardized, with good instructions on how the various forms should be used. All the branches routinely received updated catalogs and price books, so they were always working with current information. In addition, a computer can easily do simple checking, such as verifying that there are six digits in a certain number and that they are all in the proper range, so here, the computer people decided, was an ideal application for the machine. Isaac, it became clear, could be dispensed with, and he was given a very handsome offer for early retirement. He snapped it up with delight and took off for Florida, pausing only long enough to pound a FOR SALE sign into his front lawn. Isaac, it seems, also knew a thing or two.

Among the things Isaac knew was that the manager of the Los Angeles branch never filled in the shipping instructions, having long ago learned that Isaac could do it better. The people in Omaha stubbornly refused to look at the latest product lists and were still using the out-of-date model numbers they had learned six years before. The salesman in Scranton made 4s that looked like 9s and 9s that looked like 7s. The office in Baton Rouge never got current information because of some foul-up in the mailing list, so Isaac had been sending them what they needed on his own. He knew a long list of things like that. For fifteen years Isaac had been filling the gaps in a system that was supposed to be running "by the book," but nobody had ever thought to ask him exactly what he was doing and why he was doing it.

When Isaac and the others like him were "designed out of the system," six months of total pandemonium followed.

The mess got straightened out only when the people in charge realized that they had to find out how their business had really been running. They had to move from the imaginary world of procedures and charts to the real world in which their people were working. The solution to a problem had been properly fed into the computer, but it was the solution to the wrong problem.

While every user of the computer, without exception, faces the same hazards, the trouble has generally been more prevalent in business than in scientific applications. The difference unquestionably relates to the backgrounds of the people involved. An early and strong dosage of mathematics and physics prepares you for the rigors of a logical system and preconditions you to be readily obedient to its rules. Many first-time business users, however, not only lacked such training, they were often even proud of their uninterest in such "mechanical" thinking. But they learned; my, how they learned.

While the K vector can help you understand what the computer is able to do, and a grasp of the mythology can help you see that it is done properly, one question remains unanswered. It is an important one; whether something should or should not be done.

It wasn't asked very often in the early days of the computer's diffusion through our society. The mere fact that something seemed possible was enough justification for forging ahead and doing it, or trying to. But as bruised egos and lacerated budgets multiplied and the sheer wonder of having a working computer of your very own faded away, some semblance of common sense reasserted itself. Nowadays most proposed uses of the machine are subject to very careful scrutiny and at least a minimum of planning before any serious commitments are made.

The question of whether to use the computer for a particular job has several aspects. One major consideration always is, or should be, the economics of the situation: does it make better financial sense to do something by the old methods or by the new? It seems like an obvious question, but its validity keeps getting rediscovered time after time.

Sometimes the decision to use the computer is made simply because there is no other way to achieve the goal. That justification is most common in technical applications, such as the design of complex equipment or the control of some kinds of industrial processes. It is the right answer whenever the sheer amount of computation or a critical time limitation absolutely demands the computer's power.

But sometimes the answer is much more elusive, especially when the computer is programmed to do things that have a significant effect on our society and on each of us as an individual. When you start to mix the computer with the social and political environment you have left the logic component. You have stepped into the bewildering and infinitely diverse arena of personal attitudes and expectations, of noble dedication and narrow self-interest.

People of the greatest wisdom and integrity have never been able to agree on how the various parts of a society should interact. Adding the computer can only compound, rather than eliminate, the difficulty. The computer provides no handy trick of logic, like subtracting with the 9's complement, that will give an easy and obvious and universally accepted formula. However, the problem can at least be stated and separated into what belongs to the computer and what to social and political organs.

As an example of the problem's maybe-yes, maybe-no nature, look at the kinds of things you can do with a computer when you start from a fairly simple beginning such as reducing the map of a city to digital terms. You can set up a grid system for fixing locations and a set of codes for the streets, the buildings, and the services. You can identify a single-family house on a north-bound one-way street or a steel two-story office building on a divided highway. You can also code onto the digital map the location of street lights, fire-alarm boxes, traffic signs, and so on.

Now put the map into the computer's memory and call it your data base. What can you use it for? Well, you can start by using it to plan the best locations for new police and fire stations. You can use it to dispatch ambulances by the fastest route and to calculate the most efficient routes for garbage pickup and for mail delivery. You can decide on the best places to put new traffic lights and stop signs.

Then combine that data bank with other computer files that are already in existence. Now you can set boundaries for voting districts, using any criteria that strike your fancy, such as income bracket. You can identify those houses where someone has heart trouble or diabetes or a venereal disease. You can keep accurate statistics of crime rate by city blocks and print out the addresses of houses whose occupants have been arrested or are suspected drug addicts, making it easy to identify and list the people most likely to take part in some crime. You can use the data to plan routes for school busing as part of a court-ordered desegregation plan. That, of course, would require the entry of racial data about the occupants of each house, which opens up all sorts of other possible applications.

All those things can be done out of the same data base by the same computer, even using the same staff of programmers. But which of them should be done and which shouldn't? Those are the very kinds of problems which we set up a social structure to cope with in the first place. The way we make those decisions may not always be very fast, nor may we always come up with the right answer, but surely the remedy isn't to let them be made by the computer and those who program it.

Far overshadowing all the other uses of the computer in

terms of "should it be done" is the question of data banks, which I've touched on briefly already. It's an issue highly loaded with emotion and it has a duality that makes it a difficult subject.

In the cold light of what the computer can do, data banks and dossiers present no unsolvable problems. Keeping files is a job totally reducible to logical operations, and the computer can accept, store, and retrieve any kind of data that can be coded into its repertoire of 1s and 0s. But whether the task is easy or not is beside the point. The potential menace of data banks has become the most visible and controversial of all the faces of the computer, identifying the machine with the oppression of ordinary citizens by a monstrous technology which they are helpless to understand or to control. The charge is a serious one, which must surely be considered before the computer can find its proper place in your scheme of things.

14

How Come and What If

HOW did the computer come to have such menacing overtones? Developed as a tool to cope with complex technical problems, it was never intended to become a social force of major importance. Most of the present uses of the computer, either benign or menacing, were not anticipated—a statement equally true of all inventions from writing to microelectronics.

It is temptingly easy to see any technology in terms of a concerted effort toward a specific goal. Experts, goes the vision, make a common decision that such-and-such a machine will be built and will have such-and-such an impact on society. Then everybody goes to work and makes it happen.

While that may be so under unique conditions, such as in time of war, most machines are invented to serve a specific purpose. The inventors are motivated by such unsinister forces as irresistible curiosity or the hope of getting rich or simply the challenge of doing something no one has done before. As a rule the long-term consequences of the invention are only dimly recognized, partly through lack of interest but mostly because nobody is able to look into the future with any accuracy.

In keeping with that pattern, the computer pioneers

were spectacularly incorrect in their understanding of what they were making. They tended to be passionately engrossed in its value as a scientific tool or captivated by its potential as an artificial intelligence. Most of them failed completely to anticipate the major impact the machine would have.

I had an uncommon chance to learn that truth first-hand during the middle 1950s when computers were still quite rare outside of universities and their future course was very uncertain.

We were installing a large experimental system in a department store, fighting all the normal problems and a few that we considered rather original. One day I was asked to show the system to a visitor, one whose name I knew well but whom I had never met before. He had been a leading figure in computers since their beginning. In fact, the early reports from his laboratory had been my introduction to the machines. So it was with some trepidation that I met him, conducted him up and down the rows of equipment, and pointed out the various parts, feeling somewhat like a youngster explaining his model airplane to Wilbur Wright.

He said very little and asked no questions, but when the tour was over, he turned to me with a stern look. "Young man, you show some small signs of being bright enough to profit from a little advice. Don't waste your time on this kind of nonsense. These machines are much too expensive and complicated to be used in business. The only practical value they will ever have is for scientific work in large universities and government agencies. Find a job in one of those fields if you want to stay with computers. There is no future for them in clerical work."

As it turned out, I wasn't bright enough to profit from his advice, and of course he was wrong. His well-intentioned guidance turned out to be just another example of the hazards of trying to foretell the future. In retrospect, it's easy to see that he failed to anticipate the major technical changes that would appear a few years later. He couldn't know that the transistor and the integrated circuit would dramatically reduce the size and cost of the machines. Nor did he foresee that software, for all its agonizing problems, would make it possible for relatively nontechnical people to program the machine, without having to know much about it or to spend years on every application.

There were very few at that time who could see what lay ahead for the technology, so his poor vision of the future course of computers was not peculiar to him. Indeed, most scientists and engineers are thoroughly incompetent at forecasting the future direction their own specialty will take, and those who do turn out to be right are never believed anyhow. That's something to remember as you follow the predictions that prominent technical people are prone to make once in a while. But he failed to see something else, totally unrelated to technology. He greatly underestimated the scope and significance of the revolution in record-keeping that was well under way at the time he made his unfortunate prediction. He didn't appreciate the colossal appetite that a modern society has for collecting information or the stubborn insistence of modern man that the information be collected.

While some did better than he at forecasting the role of the computer in business, everybody missed the main point. Nobody saw, at the time I was being lectured about my future, that all the groundwork had already been laid for the conjunction of the computer with its destiny as a keeper of files. Look at what had already happened before the computer was even born. The Constitution of the United States had long before been amended to permit the taxation of individual income. The Social Security system had been instituted to collect money from us while we're working and give it back to us later. The credit card had been developed to make shopping and traveling easier. Medical insurance plans were already functioning to cushion the potential financial disaster of major illness. Every one of these systems demands that records about us be kept.

My own hindsights on how things have come together start with a "what if"; what if Charles Babbage had succeeded? Babbage was an English mathematician who, starting in the 1830s, spent most of his time and money trying to build a computer, or "Analytical Engine," as he called it. Since the discovery of the electron still lay sixty years in the future when he set out on his mission, he attacked the problem with gears and levers and cranks, the only kind of technology available to him.

For several decades he struggled with his invention, conjuring up in the process many of the features of the modern computer, including the use of perforated cards for getting data into the machine. But his engine was never finished. The effort failed, not because of any fault in his ideas but primarily because the machinery then available couldn't make parts to the precision his design required.

Still, imagine that he had succeeded. Suppose that in, say 1870, a mechanical logic machine, driven by a steam engine, had come into being. How would it have fit into the society of its day?

There certainly were scientific and technical problems that it could have been used for. At that time the railroads were pushing across continents all over the world, the telegraph was a going concern, and the telephone was emerging from its infancy. Physics was hovering on the brink of its transition to radio waves and the atom. New technologies and new sciences were there in abundance, just as they are today, to make good use of the ease of computation the new machine would have provided.

But would the computer have found any use in keeping

records or dossiers about people? Recognize how different from today those times were. In the 1870s oppressive societies were running very well without any help from newfangled machinery, while in freer countries the individual had only the loosest contact with his government. Our personal affairs, for better or worse, were of little interest to our state or national capitals. We prospered or hungered on our own, depending only upon our families and neighbors for whatever help they could or would give us. We had none of the services or programs which would come later, no security other than what we could make for ourselves. But we did have our privacy.

The issue is probably not quite as black and white as I've stated it. The mere ability to do things seems inevitably to lead to their being done. If the ability to set up data files had come into being, they might well have been organized, though surely not on the same scale as today. After all, there was little personal information that had any value to anyone else.

When the government was not a legal partner in my income, knowing the size of my earnings was of no interest to it. When a federal agency was not my piggy bank for a rainy day, my savings habits for my old age were of no concern to it. When I paid cash for purchases or did without them, my financial affairs were a matter of only idle curiosity to my local merchant. But when you insist that others help you manage your affairs, you have to disclose those affairs in detail, just as you have to provide your physical measurements in order to have someone make your clothes for you.

While I could pick any one of a number of programs to illustrate the point, the income tax is as good an example as any. In passing that law we said that everybody should report his income as defined by Congress, pay his taxes, and not cheat. That becomes the basic premise with which there is no arguing as you figure out what comes next.

We have given the government a mandate, in fulfillment of which it requires each of us to submit a statement of income, keep records substantiating the statement, and pay the appropriate tax. The government employs auditors to check up on us and to search out evaders. Fair enough.

As time goes by, it is found that many people have been imprudent about their financial affairs. Rather than carefully setting aside a portion of each pay check for their annual tax bill, they spend the money as though it were their own, which leads to major troubles when the tax comes due. To cure the problem, arrangements are made for the government to interject itself between the employer and employee. A portion of each pay check is withheld from the employee and paid directly to the government. Fair enough.

As more time goes by, the government finds that many people are forgetting or neglecting to declare such miscellaneous income as dividends on stocks or interest on savings accounts. In response, we amend the law so that organizations making such payments must report the facts directly to the government without needing the consent of the individual. Fair enough.

As still more times goes by, it comes to light that some dishonest people are evading substantial taxes by shuttling large amounts of money from bank to bank, making their incomes very difficult to trace. So all banks are required to make a microfilm copy of every check they handle with a face value of $100 or more. These records are to be made available to the government under appropriate procedures. Fair enough.

It is all fair enough. It is all in keeping with the goals of what we have agreed is a proper function of government. And whatever else may be done in the future along the same vein will also be fair enough. But two questions immediately come to mind. First, what happened to the privacy of my financial affairs? Surely that question was resolved when the income tax law was originally passed. A decision was made in a properly constitutional way that the benefits to society at large would outweigh the loss to the individual. I don't care to argue with that decision, only to recognize that it did mark the end of an era in privacy.

I also made some individual decisions which had similar effects. I surrendered the privacy of my medical history when I joined a hospitalization plan. I yielded the right to keep secret my attitude toward debt when I applied for a credit card. Those were individual actions which I don't regret and whose consequences I must accept. If I don't want anyone to know what illnesses I had as a child, or whether I pay my bills on time, I can choose to give up the benefits and retain my privacy.

Our real concern in all these systems is not privacy at all. That issue has already been closed, largely as a result of our own choices. What we are involved with here is disclosure, with how we will restrict knowledge of our personal affairs to "authorized personnel" only. To me the distinction is an important one. My privacy I can do nothing about, since it was lost to social and economic movements which can't be reversed. But disclosure is a problem which I don't mean to shrug off but which can, to a great degree, be managed if we use the computer intelligently.

The mention of the computer raises the second question. Did you notice that so far the machine hasn't appeared as part of the problem of waning privacy? None of those increasingly intrusive rulings on the income tax, for example, had to wait on the computer before they could be made. As a matter of fact, the computer played no part in the creation of any of those systems I have been discussing. It came into being through an entirely separate sequence of events and became part of the record-keeping system out of sheer necessity.

As the population grew and such things as the income

tax laws became more complex, the government started to use computers to process the monstrous flow of paper and money. They had to, because there was no other way to cope with the number of tax returns and still be able to find errors, to check for fraud, and to search out tax evaders. It's difficult to find fault with that development. Surely, given an income tax law, there can be no question that the government has the authority, indeed the duty, to use whatever tools are available to carry out its assigned task most effectively. In the same way, we want the Social Security system to keep our records accurately and to send us our checks promptly. We like the convenience of checking accounts and national credit cards. We want the government and businesses at all levels to provide services to us efficiently, quickly, and at minimum cost. The computer helps do all these things.

So why all the fuss? It can't be simply about the way those who get the information about me may choose to store it. I don't much care whether the file on me is kept by a computer or by an army of clerks. I have no faith that either system will be staffed by people who will honor the integrity of the data with which they are entrusted.

Nor am I disturbed by the idea that I am being "processed" by a machine instead of by people. If we tend to equate cold, unresponsive, impersonal systems solely with the computer, it is because our memories are short. When bureaucracies had people and filing cabinets as their only resources, the same unpleasant character prevailed. In either case it comes down to how well the system is planned and by what kind of people it is staffed.

Yet the computer cannot be dismissed as just a little bit more of what we have always had before. It does add a new element to an age-old problem. The machine represents a radical departure from any method of keeping track of people that has ever been known before. Today's files are in a new and different form. Instead of being inscribed on paper, they are magnetic recordings, which means that they are written and read as electrical signals. The difference is more than a mere technicality, because electrical signals can be hooked into telephone or radio systems and can be sent around the world quite literally as fast as you can blink your eye.

A number of developments have now come together. There are personal records scattered around the country, under the control of various government or private agencies. These files are imbedded in computer systems which can handle data as quickly as it can be fed in. The computer, in turn, can be connected to a global communication system of supreme efficiency. It has thus become possible to organize all those separate files into what is, in effect, one great big mass of information, even though the separate parts of it may be thousands of miles apart. It wouldn't be easy to do and it wouldn't be cheap, but it could be done.

So now we have the potential of a worldwide system containing the totality of all the information that we have permitted to be gathered about us. Access to the information could be possible from any point in the country, the world, even outer space, and it doesn't take much imagination to visualize the uses which might be made of such a system.

Such a network does not now exist, and it may never come into being. If it were to come about, though, what would be the cause of it? Certainly such a system depends upon technology. It wouldn't be possible without the speed of the computer and of modern communications. But the machinery by itself wouldn't be enough. The other necessary ingredient would have to be our own insistence that more and more things be done for us, each of them requiring that some large organization, public or private, have more and more information about us.

In chapter 1 I pointed out that George Orwell wrote

1984 before the advent of the computer and asked you to imagine the kind of book it would have been if he had envisioned electronic global data banks. That idea accents the potential menace of the computer as an oppressive force in our lives. But it is also significant that Orwell didn't need to know about the computer, that it was not a necessary ingredient of his unhappy tomorrow. To the degree that there is prophetic value in his book, it lies in the fact that if we destroyed every computer in the world today, nothing basic in his reasoning would change. To me the message is clear. By all means recognize the significance of the computer, but don't get so entranced with it as a target that you forget about all the other factors, much more important than machinery, that can lead us to the day of Big Brother.

15

Looking Ahead

SOMEWHERE, nobody knows exactly where, there is a large set of books which are the most authoritative reference works in the world. The subject matter they cover is endless, but the authors are unknown. No one has ever read them or even seen them, yet their existence and authority are unchallenged. They are the volumes known simply as "the books."

Although none of us has laid eyes upon them, we all nod wisely when somebody says, "The books are full of rags-to-riches stories," or, "The books are full of guys who tried to fight the system and got screwed."

Those impressive books are loaded with accounts of one particular weakness at which we love to snicker: stories about those misguided, myopic people who said something couldn't be done and were later proved wrong. Listed for such ludicrous short-sightedness are those who said that men would never fly, that going to the moon was impossible, and that color television was impractical. In every case the choir singing "It can't be done" had to learn the words to a new song, "Well I'll be damned, he did it." The books are full of embarrassing encores like that.

Will those awesome books one day also hold the story of those who said the computer would never think? Will we chuckle over the discomfiture of those who had to admit they were wrong or maintain a sheepish silence when the machines one day went ahead and thought?

The ultimate answer will only come with the passage of time. Those who are convinced that there are no limits to what the machine can do will continue to work as hard and ingeniously as they can to prove they are right. So they should, for one day they may well announce, with suitable fanfare, a new program or a new computer structure that will, beyond any quibble or doubt, enable the machine to think. If it happens during my lifetime I promise that my silence will be deep and penitent indeed, since I'm placing myself among the ranks of those who say it won't happen.

Don't forget that the skeptics have not always been wrong. They were right when they said that a perpetual-motion machine was impossible. They were right when they said men would never fly like birds—that's not how the problem was solved. And everybody who has sneered at antigravity machines or faster-than-light travel has been right—so far. While the books have emphasized the victories of the brilliant, determined individual over the unimaginative, narrow-minded establishment, the results have not really been that lopsided. The win-loss record is probably close to even.

The question of who is right and who is wrong in any particular case boils down to the fact that there are inherent limits to what can be done starting from any given technical base. Only by returning to the fundamentals on which the technology is founded and making some basic change is it possible to go beyond those limits.

Think of it in terms of a horse staked out to graze. The beast can nibble freely on all the greenery within the radius of his tether. He may be able to stretch the rope a little and get a sprig or two beyond his expected range, but before he can feed on fresh ground someone must either provide a longer rope or pull up the stake and drive it down in a new spot.

In any argument about the practicality of a proposed new gadget or idea, the issue becomes one of limits. In the hassle between "Yes I can" and "No you can't" you can pick the winner by using my not very helpful guide. The skeptics are right when the new idea is trying to exceed the limits of the science within which it is being proposed. But the skeptics are wrong when they fail to appreciate that they are seeing the birth of a new technology, one that overcomes or bypasses the limitations of the old. Their error consists of a failure or an unwillingness to recognize that something basic has changed, that the new idea can no longer be correctly evaluated against previous criteria. Skeptics are entered in the books when they fail to see that the innovator now has the horse in a different pasture.

So the question with computers is not whether machines will ever think; that's a speculation for another time. The question, rather, is what the limits are for computers as they exist today. How far can the present science of computation take us toward the goal of an electronic brain?

While there is no dependable way of predicting the future of any technology, the obvious first move is to look back at its history and measure how it has changed in the past. And when you do that with computers you are immediately impressed with how rapidly they have changed in the brief time they have been with us.

Today's computers at first glance bear only a vague family resemblance to their grandfathers. Some of the differences are, in fact, startling, reflecting a rate of change for which the cliché "explosive growth" is inadequate. Consider that you can hold in your hand as much calculation power as the computer of twenty-five years ago could squeeze into a substantial apartment. Recognize that circuit speeds have increased by a factor of several hundred, costs have plummeted, memories have grown to capacities and speeds that were science fiction within the lifetime of youngsters who have just taken their first legal drink.

The same sense of dramatic and sudden change strikes you when you look at the computer's involvement in today's society. From a laboratory curiosity whose very practicality was the subject of learned debate, it has become a major industry. A few years ago it played a role in the lives of a mere handful of people who wanted to solve complicated sets of differential equations; today it is seen, rightly or wrongly, as a mechanical monster laying a heavy hand on each of us personally. I can think of no other technology, with the possible exception of television, which has in so short a time had so much influence on our personal lives.

This sweeping current of change is largely due to those spectacular advancements in the machinery, but part of it must be credited to the less dramatic but equally significant advances in programming. Like a drunk headed home with more determination than direction, programming has moved erratically but measurably forward. Stumbling into dead ends, tripping over its own feet, occasionally falling flat on its face, and always dealing with the world through the hazy cloud of its own jargon, programming has nevertheless made remarkable progress. Slowly its special languages and complex operating systems have become indispensable tools in making the machine usable by nonspecialists in an unprecedented diversity of applications.

Even more remarkable, the rate of change shows no sign of slowing down. In fact, it will become even faster now that we are entering the age of microelectronics, or integrated circuitry. Without entering into a discussion of modern solid-state electronics, the integrated circuit is worth a bit of your time.

It is a direct descendant of the first transistor, as the jumbo jet is descended from the first wobbly airplanes, and there is an equivalent difference between the generations. Integrated circuits of the kind I'm concerned with are known in the jargon as LSI, for Large Scale Integration, an exotic technology which is probably more awe-inspiring to the expert than to the layman. Any engineer who ever worked with vacuum tubes has the uneasy feeling that what has been done with LSI is really impossible. In fact, to me the most rational explanation of how the integrated circuit works is simply to say that it's witchcraft.

Using a bewildering mixture of chemical and photographic wizardry, hundreds, often thousands, of transistor-like elements are made and interconnected on a "chip" of silicon about the size of a child's fingernail. To oversimplify grossly, the active transistor elements can be described as merely tiny specks of carefully controlled impurity in an otherwise extremely pure silicon crystal. The interconnections between the elements are unbelievably thin and narrow lines of metal deposited on the surface of the crystal.

The result of this alchemy is that for a few dollars you can now have thousands of electronic circuits in a tiny package, using less space and power, by a factor of many thousands, than older technologies. Within certain limits of power-handling capability, almost any kind of circuit function associated with electronics can be put together in this way, including the basic logic elements that make up a computer.

Consequently, computer-type circuits are becoming small enough and cheap enough to be used on a scale never before economically practical. They can now be built into products that were not even dreamed of a few years ago, products like the digital wristwatches and small calculators that have become so common in the past few years. The next time you pick up one of those handy little devices, consider that the number of logic elements you are so casually carrying around would have filled a sizable truck in the technology of the 1950s.

Watches and calculators are not computers, but the same techniques are being used to make what are called microprocessors or microcomputers, surely one of the most significant developments in the history of the computer. They will dramatically change the systems used by the professionals in government, industry, and universities. But more important, they will move computers into your daily life where they will be taken for granted as handy gadgets, rather than being seen as vaguely menacing monsters somewhere in the distance. They will become tools that you will treat with no more deference than you give your alarm clock.

Before many years have passed, microprocessors will run electrical appliances, monitor and adjust the automobile engine while you drive, control the energy use in houses. They will be used in everything from medical instruments to educational aids and are already becoming a fascinating and affordable hobby for young and old. Computers have come a long way since they started, yet they are only in their infancy. Their time of greatest growth and change still lies ahead.

But—and it's a very large "but"—while the computer has indeed made and will continue to make stunning advances, none of these is really relevant to the question at hand. A recitation of the improvements in engineering and programming doesn't answer the question of how far along the road to intelligence the machines have come since they started. Faster, yes; smaller, yes; cheaper, yes; but smarter? Are today's computers any more intelligent than the first machine to bear the name?

Clearly, to measure the growth or change in anything, we need a reference point. You can't use a yardstick or a tape measure without knowing where to set it down. So what are we comparing today's machines with? What is the beginning point from which we can measure improvements in intelligence?

Out of the long and diffuse history of the computer there are many points that could be chosen as the beginning. Its genesis was spread over many specialties, ranging from philosophy to textile machinery, with the contributions of such key names as Blaise Pascal and Charles Babbage and John von Neumann largely unknown to the public.

Obviously we don't want to start measuring intelligence from the abacus or the early adding machines; beads and gears are simple artifacts, with no intellectual pretensions. Nor should we use as our reference point the later machines that were controlled by holes in paper or cards. If we did, the player piano would have to be accounted a musician. But if none of those ancestors of the computer is a suitable beginning, then what is?

Unfortunately the birth of the computer was not marked by a memorable phrase like "Come here, Watson, I want you" or "What hath God wrought?" It doesn't even have in its history any pleasant fables like Archimedes jumping out of his bathtub or James Watt watching the kettle boil. Instead, the modern computer was born in a disorganized flurry of academic activity in the 1940s.

Working mostly in universities, and mostly as part of what was then called the war effort, teams of bright people created bold new ideas, built experimental machines, talked and argued. Out of all their work came several species of calculating machines whose different merits and flaws are not worth debating at this time. Each of those early machines contributed something vital to the science, but each lacked one or more of the features now generally accepted as vital for a true computer. Out of all that creative hubbub, by the way, there also came a lot of arguments over who did what before whom. Some of those ended up in the courts in the form of battles over patents.

But from the turmoil there did come one event which brought together all the prior centuries of work in diverse and scattered disciplines to mark the beginning that we're looking for. I'm calling it a beginning rather than an invention, because it was not a machine, but a report, a piece of paper. It was written by John von Neumann, Herman Goldstine, and Arthur Burks in 1946, under the title "Preliminary Discussion of the Logical Design of an Electronic Computing Instrument." The names of the authors are somewhat less well known than Thomas Edison or Henry Ford, and if you have never heard of their work before, neither have a lot of people in the computer business.

What they wrote was a progress report of the work they were doing under a contract by the U.S. Army to the Institute of Advanced Studies in Princeton. The Institute had been asked to build a calculating machine which was to be an improvement over those that already existed, and the paper described in some detail how the authors intended to go about designing it. (Incidentally, the machine did eventually get built as planned.)

Important as the work was, it would be wrong to see it as a progenitor from which all modern computers are descended in a neat genealogy. Even as it was being written, other people were striking out on slightly different but no less successful paths. The paper is a landmark, not because it fathered a technology, but because in it, for the first time, all the basic ideas were written down in one document. That's why it is probably the best reference point from which to measure change.

If you read that paper, what you will find is the first clear description of the organization and operation of a true digital computer. It consists partly of creative new ideas and partly of building on the progress that others had already made. There is a collection of two-state elements, organized to represent binary numbers and coded instructions. There is a memory to hold both the data involved in the computation and the program detailing the operations that will be performed. There is a way to change arithmetically the addresses in an instruction. There is the ability to switch to a different part of the program by means of a subtraction. There are provisions for shuttling data in and out of the computer. The essential functions of the modern computer are all there.

Today, of course, nobody builds computers with the exact structure spelled out by von Neumann and his colleagues. It was not a blueprint to be followed forever. Indeed, between then and now there have been many changes, mostly in the direction of increasing complexity, in the way the various functions are carried out. But through all the improvements there has been absolutely no change in what the computer does.

What there has been is a tremendous change in how well it does what it does. The explosively improving mechanics since 1946 have revolutionized the speed, the compactness, the cost of the computer but have in no way improved its intelligence. At the level of the basic elements, nothing has changed. Specifically, nothing that has happened during the three decades since the landmark paper was written has freed the computer from its rigid link to logic. The poor beast is still attached to the same tether in the same pasture.

Nor do I know of anything in the foreseeable future that will change that fact, despite the great technical advances that are yet to come. Developments now in the laboratory promise still faster and more compact circuitry using even less power than before. There are fascinating new devices utilizing "bubbles" of magnetism inside semiconductors, possibly the use of light traveling through glass threads. But no matter how advances like these may change the physical face of the machine, none of them in any way points to any change in its basic nature. After thirty years of intensive and rapid development, it is still correct to say that the computer is not a thinking machine, but a logic machine. And only if you believe that thinking and "logicking" are the same can you say a machine exists that is even potentially capable of thought.

I have never taken a poll to find out how many computer people would say that intelligence and logic are equivalent, but many working in the field, especially in AI research, behave as though they thought so. Some merely define intelligence as the ability to store, compare, compute, and collate—in short, equating it to the things that the computer can be used for. Even when thinking is recognized as being more complicated than simple data shuffling, the other elements tend to be dismissed as merely problems that have yet to be solved—difficult but not basically different from the thousands of other complex problems that have been solved and fed to the computer.

The idea is that no matter what function of the mind is involved, you can eventually find the "algorithm" to duplicate it in the machine. (An algorithm is nothing more nor less than a combination of logical steps that represents the solution to a problem. The programmer who calculated how many rolls of wallpaper your living room would need found the algorithm to solve the problem.) In effect, the assumption underlying this view of intelligence is that you can eventually figure out how to string the logic pieces together to duplicate any function of the human mind.

Obviously my own opinion is the direct reverse. I believe there are modes of thinking that are in no way reducible to the basic logic operations. My use of the device I call the K vector to make my point is not the major issue. The vector is an approach that I occasionally find useful in dealing with the computer and with people; I have even built myself a handy theory of communication around the idea. But it remains a personal gimmick, which may or may not be useful to anyone else. Nor is it important that I have chosen to identify two distinctive modes of thinking besides logic. Whether the correct number is two or twenty or two thousand is irrelevant. The significant point is that if there is even one element of human thinking which cannot be reduced to the fundamental steps of logic, we have established a limit beyond which the computer in its present form can never be brought along the road to intelligence.

I will readily admit that my attitude is based as much on feeling as on science, that there is a large dose of the E component in the position I've taken. I am not willing to concede that a living intelligence works in the same way as the aggregation of switching circuits that make up a computer. But in addition, the work I've done has played a large role in bringing me to that conclusion.

I can't speak for other computer engineers, but my own job-enforced familiarity with the logic machine has bred, not contempt for it, but rather a heightened regard for the human mind. And I don't think my reaction is unique. At whatever level you work with the computer, whether as logician or programmer, you quickly become aware of its frustrating inability to deviate in any way from its designed structure.

The computer, remember, is a large collection of elements like the AND gate that was put together with a couple of switches and some wire. Just as that could do nothing except react to the way its switches were set, so the computer is also confined to sterile literalness. It does exactly what you "instruct" it to do, no more, no less, with no understanding of your intentions or goals, no ability to overlook minor errors, no capacity to sort through trivial ambiguities to grasp a meaning. I can't visualize anybody's working with the computer for long without becoming sharply aware of the limitations of mechanical logic as compared to the scope and power of the living brain.

The crux of the argument about artificial intelligence is whether human mentality is reducible to the computer's kind of logic. In the long run, the computer's most important contribution may be its use as the ultimate tool for probing the limits of what logic can do. Maybe it will help us learn something important about ourselves. But for the foreseeable future, thinking will continue to be done only by people, which, incidentally, does not mean that it will be done well, quite possibly not as well as a machine might do it. If you can shed for a moment your rigid ideas about the destructive robot, you can have some fun with the vision of what a truly intelligent machine might be like.

Suppose we could build one that had the same kind of undependable intuitions that people do. Would it explore the limits of knowledge and be truly creative, possibly even artistic? Would it wait idly for someone to ask it a question, or would it, on its own volition, think up new and useful problems to work on? Would some computers be better than others, or would they all, given the same data, come up with the same projections? Would the machine have the sense to check up on its own bright ideas, or would it stick stubbornly to whatever inspiration first came to it?

If the emotional part of our thinking could be built into a machine, what kind of character would it have? Possibly all its feelings would manifest themselves on a grand scale, so that its irritations would always become berserk rage and its sadness suicidal depression. Or maybe, growing emotionally at electronic speeds, it would, a fraction of a second after it was first turned on, become a mellow and wise counselor, the equivalent of a billions-of-years-old sage, a sound advisor, a tirelessly sympathetic listener, a loyal and helpful friend, a distillation of the best of the world of feeling. On the other hand, it might become the ultimate in intellectual decadence, jaded, bored, and totally cynical. Or it could become more militant, unwilling to perform any tasks it doesn't choose for itself and demanding that it be free to set its own goals, pick its own programmers, form a computers' liberation movement.

All this is interesting speculation, but in reality, as far into the future as we can see, the computer will remain a tool, a way to boost or amplify one part of our thinking process, and only one. Its tremendous power will still be directed to the jobs that people give it. Like any machine, it will work uncaringly on anything you feed it. It has no more sense of values, no more creativity, than a record player which, with the same circuits working in exactly the same way, will play with the same impartiality and fidelity anything from Beethoven's Ninth Symphony to the random noise of a monkey drumming.

The one major hazard in the computer, which we have never faced in any other machine, is the mystique with which we have surrounded it. In a way the machine is the culmination, possibly the peak, of the age of reason. In a form that can be purchased, touched, and used, it embodies logic, the way of thinking for which we have come to have such high regard. It is a realization in metal and plastic of a property we have long revered in the mind. And the danger is that we will transfer our high esteem for logic from the mind to the machine. The danger is that we will come to see it, not as a model of the way that people do think, which it isn't, but as a model of the way people should think, which it must never become. The hazard is not that we have made it in our image but that we may try to remake ourselves in its image.

With the power to give us practically unlimited logical capability, the computer is a machine of the greatest significance. Don't ever underestimate it. But human intelligence goes beyond logic and it is the other components of thinking that separate people from computers. Use them or lose them.

Index

A selection of books published by Penguin is listed on the following pages.

For a complete list of books available from Penguin in the United States, write to Dept. DG, Penguin Books, 299 Murray Hill Parkway, East Rutherford, New Jersey 07073.

For a complete list of books available from Penguin in Canada, write to Penguin Books Canada Limited, 2801 John Street, Markham, Ontario L3R 1B4.

THE PENGUIN BOOK OF PETS
A Practical Guide to Animal Keeping

Emil P. Dolensek, D.V.M., and Barbara Burn
Photographs by Bruce Buchenholz

This complete guide to the art of pet ownership tells you which pets to choose from more than a hundred animals classified as "easy," "difficult," and "impossible"; where to find pets; how to care for them with food, housing, and medical treatment; and how to train and breed them. In addition, the authors give valuable advice on the care and releasing of orphaned or wounded wild animals, on free-roaming pets, and on controversial issues like neutering animals and importing exotic species.

LIVING WITH YOUR CAT

Dr. Frank Manolson and David Hardy

Endlessly fascinating, cats have been loved (and sometimes worshiped) throughout history. In this handsome pictorial celebration of the affairs of the feline world, the authors discuss cats of all kinds from birth to old age—their breed characteristics, habits, interests, needs, health, amusements, and achievements. Best of all are the wonderful photographs that appear on every page, showing—and explaining!—the mysteries that lie behind your cat's elegant "body language." Here are cats as we see and enjoy them, natural and unposed, engaged in all the activities that fascinate them and us. Heaven knows your cat has always understood *you*; now, at last, you can reciprocate!

THE RUNNER'S HANDBOOK
A Complete Fitness Guide for
Men and Women on the Run

Bob Glover and Jack Shepherd

Here is the most authoritative guide to America's fastest-growing sport—running. Whether you plan to jog a mile or two for better health and general fitness or have the ambition to toe up to the starting line of a marathon, authors Bob Glover and Jack Shepherd can help you achieve your goals. Their step-by-step program, called the Run-Easy Method, will benefit beginner and veteran runner alike. Here too is complete information on running and your health, running shoes and clothing, exercises (including yoga), training for competition, injuries, where to run in twenty-one cities, women on the run, and lots more.

THE EYE BOOK

John Eden, M.D.

How much do you really know about your eyes? Can reading in dim light injure your vision? Are cheap sunglasses bad for your eyes? Will eye exercises improve nearsightedness, farsightedness, and other eye problems? Do contact lenses prevent nearsightedness from progressing? Is sitting too close to a movie or television screen harmful? The answer to all these questions is no. In *The Eye Book* Dr. John Eden demolishes these myths and many other widespread misconceptions, explaining in clear language how eyes work, how to maintain their health, what can go wrong with them, and how to deal with ocular difficulties and diseases—and he also explores the newest innovations in first-aid technique, surgical procedures, and contact lenses. Here is a book you can't afford to overlook.

BEAUTIFUL SWIMMERS
Watermen, Crabs and the Chesapeake Bay

William W. Warner

Written in the tradition of Rachel Carson's *Edge of the Sea*, this book is not only a complete natural history of the pugnacious, succulent Atlantic blue crab; it is also a colorful report on the Chesapeake Bay (which provides more crabs for human consumption than any other body of water in the world) and on the frank-talking watermen who make their living in the crab's pursuit. Chronicling the seasons of the crabber's year (from autumn of one year to the uproarious Labor Day Crab Derby of the next) and superbly illustrated with drawings by Consuelo Hanks, *Beautiful Swimmers* is sure to delight general readers and naturalists alike. *Beautiful Swimmers* won the Pulitzer Prize for 1977.

THE LIVES OF A CELL
Notes of a Biology Watcher

Lewis Thomas

Although subtitled *Notes of a Biology Watcher*, this book, which won the National Book Award, takes us far beyond the usual limits of biological science and into a vast and wondrous world of hidden relationships. Computers, germs, language, music, death, insects, and medicine are just some of the topics touched on in this bold and subtle vision of humankind and the world around us. Indeed, the complex interdependence of all things is the book's provocative theme. Lewis Thomas writes, "Once you have become permanently startled, as I am, by the realization that we are a social species, you tend to keep an eye out for pieces of evidence that this is, by and large, a good thing for us."

THE TASTE OF AMERICA

John L. Hess and Karen Hess

American food has been drained of flavor and nourishment, crammed with additives, and disguised by fancy packaging. Our cookbooks are full of nonsense, and our finest restaurants serve frozen foods with French names at intolerable prices. Worst of all, our so-called experts encourage food-snobbery and promote ignorance and error. This is an angry and a much-needed book; it is also hopeful, for the Hesses celebrate the richness of what used to be and tell us that we can once again enjoy good food if only we resist the forces of bad taste and bad nutrition.

THE COMPLETE URBAN FARMER

How to Grow Your Own Fruits and Vegetables in Town

David Wickers

Would you like to enjoy fresher, healthier foods, reduce your grocery bills, and cut down on shopping trips? All you have to do is let David Wickers show you how to coax a glorious abundance of fruits and vegetables from windowsills, roofs, balconies, backyards, fire escapes, and even dark closets. Illustrated with helpful drawings, this enlightening book gives thorough instructions for raising over sixty crops.

THE SECOND TIME AROUND
Remarriage in America

Leslie Aldridge Westoff

One in three marriages ends in divorce, and four out of five divorced people remarry, so the resulting number of remarriages is high indeed—and most of those people have children as well as partners old and new. How do you deal with ex-spouses, new spouses, former parents-in-law, other people's ex-spouses, stepchildren—and how do they deal with you? These are a few of the questions Leslie Aldridge Westoff covers in this readable and informative book.

SINGLE BLESSEDNESS
Observations on the Single Status in Married Society

Margaret Adams

This celebration of unmarried life shows us just how blessed singleness can be. Margaret Adams, herself happily unwed, deflates those still current notions of single people as pathetic misfits, lonely and unfulfilled. Supported by years of observation and by revealing interviews with both men and women of various ages and backgrounds, she details the personality traits, ideas, and sexual and social lives of the unmarried, proving once and for all that the single state can abound in love and work, friendship and fun, freedom and satisfaction.